British and Catholic?

Cultural Identity Studies

Volume 27

Edited by
Helen Chambers

PETER LANG
Oxford · Bern · Berlin · Bruxelles · Frankfurt am Main · New York · Wien

Martin Potter

British and Catholic?

National and Religious Identity in the Work of
David Jones, Evelyn Waugh and Muriel Spark

PETER LANG

Oxford · Bern · Berlin · Bruxelles · Frankfurt am Main · New York · Wien

Bibliographic information published by Die Deutsche Nationalbibliothek.
Die Deutsche Nationalbibliothek lists this publication in the Deutsche National-
bibliografie; detailed bibliographic data is available on the Internet at
http://dnb.d-nb.de.

A catalogue record for this book is available from the British Library.

Library of Congress Control Number: 2013936376

Cover image: Keble College Chapel, University of Oxford © Martin Potter.

ISSN 1661-3252
ISBN 978-3-0343-0860-1

© Peter Lang AG, International Academic Publishers, Bern 2013
Hochfeldstrasse 32, CH-3012 Bern, Switzerland
info@peterlang.com, www.peterlang.com, www.peterlang.net

All rights reserved.
All parts of this publication are protected by copyright.
Any utilisation outside the strict limits of the copyright law, without the permission
of the publisher, is forbidden and liable to prosecution.
This applies in particular to reproductions, translations, microfilming, and storage
and processing in electronic retrieval systems.

Printed in Germany

Contents

Acknowledgements — vii

Introduction — 1

CHAPTER 1
David Jones: Sacramentality and National History — 9

CHAPTER 2
Evelyn Waugh: The Material and the Spiritual — 55

CHAPTER 3
Muriel Spark: Layers of Identity — 89

CHAPTER 4
Alternative Approaches: G. K. Chesterton and Graham Greene — 125

Conclusion — 137

Bibliography — 143

Index — 151

Acknowledgements

Much of the research for this book was done at the Bodleian Library in Oxford, so I would like to acknowledge the staff there for their assistance. I would also like to thank Laurel Plapp and the team at Peter Lang for their help and advice. I am grateful to my mother for her constant support.

Introduction

Since the Reformation British Catholics have lived as a minority in Britain, but during the nineteenth and, especially, twentieth centuries Catholic writers played a surprisingly prominent role in British literary life. The aim of this study is to examine the attitude to British identity exhibited by three twentieth-century British writers, focusing on works of theirs particularly concerned with the problematics of being British and Catholic, and to propose that they develop a theory of how British Catholic identity can be conceived and of how the British and Catholic elements can be reconciled, and that this draws on their Catholic intellectual background.

David Jones, Evelyn Waugh and Muriel Spark have been chosen for comparison in this study because they all develop, in an interesting and parallel way, a theory of British Catholic identity, which is implicit in some of their works, a theory which emphasizes harmony and transcends the potential conflict. Not all twentieth-century British Catholic writers have approached the topic of nationality in the same way, and the cases of G. K. Chesterton and Graham Greene will also be discussed, as writers for whom the issue of nationality in the context of British Catholicism is important. These, however, do not employ the same integrating theory that, it will be argued, Jones, Waugh and Spark do. In the chapter on David Jones, discussions of three important volumes of his poetic work have been included – his work on the First World War *In Parenthesis*, his long, arguably epic, poem *The Anathemata*, and his late collection of shorter poems and fragments, *The Sleeping Lord and Other Fragments* – as well as the two published volumes of his essayistic work, *Epoch and Artist* and *The Dying Gaul*. This comprises the greater part of his published written work. In the case of the other two writers it has been possible to be more selective – from Waugh's oeuvre his novel *Helena* and the novel trilogy *Sword of Honour* are most relevant, while briefer discussions of *Brideshead Revisited*, as well as of selected travel writing, and his biography of Edmund

Campion are included. Most relevant among Spark's works are the novel *The Mandelbaum Gate*, her autobiography *Curriculum Vitae* and the short story 'The Gentile Jewesses', while the novel *The Prime of Miss Jean Brodie* also deserves brief consideration in this context. In concentrating on these, the study is focusing on works which are concerned with the issue of British Catholic identity to a significant extent, throughout their whole length. The more extensive task of tracking down every reference and allusion to the theme throughout the entire oeuvres of the writers has not been attempted.

A characteristic widely associated with British Catholic literature is a sense of alienation from the majority culture. Thomas Woodman observes that Catholics have been accustomed to regard themselves as an alien minority, and that British Catholic writers have aimed at opposing the 'pelagianism' of British society.[1] Richard Griffiths notes that English Catholic novelists have often written about what differentiates Catholicism from Anglicanism, many of them coming from Anglican backgrounds, whereas Scottish Catholic novelists seek to distinguish Catholicism from Calvinism.[2] Poitou, writing about Spark's novel, *The Mandelbaum Gate*, declares, 'Dans une Angleterre où les luttes anciennes ont laissé des séquelles, le catholicisme est presque l'Autre par excellence'.[3] Against the background of this widely recognized sense of alienation, deriving from the post-Reformation anti-Catholic penal laws, and popular prejudice, and arguably

---

[1] Thomas Woodman, *Faithful Fictions: The Catholic Novel in British Literature* (Milton Keynes: Open University Press, 1991), xiii. See also Gene Kellogg, *The Vital Tradition: The Catholic Novel in a Period of Convergence* (Chicago: Loyola University Press, 1970), 220, who argues that opposition to mainstream Protestant society provides the creative inspiration for British Catholic novelists.

[2] Richard Griffiths, *The Pen and the Cross: Catholicism and English Literature 1850–2000* (London: Continuum, 2010), 136–8.

[3] 'In an England in which the old struggles have left their mark, Catholicism is almost the Other *par excellence*'. (my translation) Marc Poitou, 'La rage d'être autre: *The Mandelbaum Gate* de Muriel Spark', *Cycnos* 2, Hiver 1985–6, 19. See also Adam Schwartz, *The Third Spring: G. K. Chesterton, Graham Greene, Christopher Dawson and David Jones* (Washington, DC: Catholic University of America Press, 2005), 1, who mentions Virginia Woolf's hostile reaction to T. S. Eliot's conversion to Anglo-Catholicism as typical of British intellectuals' attitudes to Catholicism at that time.

surviving beyond Catholic emancipation in the late eighteenth and early nineteenth centuries well into the twentieth century, Jones, Waugh and Spark seek, in the works I shall examine, a way of rehabilitating Catholicism as part of British culture, even of demonstrating that Catholicism is an integral element in British culture for historical reasons, however anti-Catholic the country may have appeared during the post-Reformation centuries.

Being Catholic in Britain is likely to impart a historical consciousness which differs from that of the majority Protestant population, especially in so far as British Catholics will have a greater awareness of the Middle Ages, this being the period when the majority of the population in Britain was Catholic. Waugh and Jones go back beyond the Middle Ages to the beginnings of Christianity in Britain, setting the novel *Helena*, in the case of Waugh, and many works in the case of Jones, in late antiquity. This period would be understood by Catholic writers as marked by the first arrival of the Catholic Church in Britain. Jones throughout his work shows a strong interest in the Middle Ages in general, as well as in the transition from late antiquity to the early Middle Ages, and he has criticized the English majority view of history for its shortsightedness in tending to regard anything from before the Reformation as very remote.[4]

One result of the characteristic British Catholic perspective on British history is a mistrust of the idea of British national identity, due to its association with post-Reformation Protestant nation-building, and there is a tendency to see nationality in terms of separate English, Scottish and Welsh nationalities, Aidan Nichols notes.[5] This separation of Britishness

---

4 See Kathleen Staudt, *At the Turn of a Civilization: David Jones and Modern Poetics* (Ann Arbor: University of Michigan Press, 1994), 153, and William Blissett, *The Long Conversation: A Memoir of David Jones* (Oxford: Oxford University Press, 1981), 105. Geraint Evans, 'Images of National Renewal in "The Sleeping Lord"', in *David Jones: Diversity in Unity: Studies in his Literary and Visual Art*, Belinda Humphrey and Anne Price-Owen, eds (Cardiff: University of Wales Press, 2000), 84, also draws attention to the fact that Jones, like his Catholic-convert friend, Welsh-language writer Saunders Lewis, preferred medieval Catholic culture to the contemporary culture in which Calvinism is the dominant religious influence.

5 Aidan Nichols, *The Realm: An Unfashionable Essay on the Conversion of England* (Oxford: Family Publications, 2008), 23–4.

into the component nationalities allows a sense of continuity with the pre-Reformation Catholic forms of the national identities of Britain. This study will show how Jones, Waugh and Spark, but especially Jones, are careful to distinguish between Englishness, Scottishness and Welshness, and refrain from endorsing a Britishness separable from a combination of the distinct component identities. Where a notion of non-compound British identity does appear in David Jones' work, it represents imperialism rather than a local identity, and Britishness as imperialism is also hinted at in Waugh's *Helena*, since for Waugh and Jones the Roman Empire can stand for the British Empire.[6]

This study will argue that the three writers have in common an approach to nationality which stresses harmonization between disparate elements rather than conflict, and that this approach is based on a philosophy of integration which underlies the thinking of all three. This integrative stance is implicit in traditional Catholic philosophy, such as Thomism,[7] and was later elaborated further by thinkers working in the Catholic tradition. The British Catholic intellectual tradition has made an important contribution to this strand of Catholic thought, particularly through the work of John Henry Newman. Newman, as part of his conversion from Anglicanism to Catholicism, struggled with Anglican criticisms of Catholic doctrine which claimed that some aspects of Catholic doctrine had been invented by the later Church, and were not part of the doctrines of the early Church, thus that the Church's doctrine had been added to, and such additions were extraneous to it. Newman's response was to write *An Essay*

---

6   See, for example, Guy Davenport, 'Stanley Spencer and David Jones', *Craft and Tradition: Essays in Honour of William Blissett*, H. B. de Groot and Alexander Legatt, eds (Calgary: University of Calgary Press, 1990), 266, who notes that, in addition to Jones, Pound, Eliot and Kipling also make the parallel between the Roman and British Empires.

7   See Aidan Nichols, *Discovering Aquinas: An Introduction to his Life, Work and Influence* (London: Darton, Longman and Todd, 2002), 165–6, on how Aquinas draws on Ancient Greek, Hebrew, and more recent Christian, Jewish and Muslim thought, and on how he sees natural philosophy as having its place under the umbrella of theology.

on the Development of Christian Doctrine, the result of a contemplation of this problem which led to his feeling able to become Catholic. In it he explained the idea that the Church's doctrine has become more explicit over the centuries, while the later explicit formulations were already implicit in the earlier beliefs. Thus the doctrines that had been added, and, according to Anglican criticism, invented, had in fact been drawn out of earlier beliefs as part of a process of harmonious development; the absence of developed doctrines in the explicit formulations of the Early Church did not mean that the Early Church would have denied them if confronted with them. Thus, also, the Church's doctrine cannot be regarded as having completed its process of development, but further developments may emerge, provided that they are implicit in the deposit of faith already held. Allied to this understanding of how the Church's doctrine has developed according to its pre-existing inner logic, rather than being changed since the Church's foundation, is the view that pre-Christian natural religious understanding is legitimate, and added to rather than contradicted by Christian revelation, as well, of course, as the view that Jewish revelation was true, and a preparation for Christian revelation. Newman expresses his understanding that converts to the Church are likely to be adding to a core of legitimate religious understanding which they already have, for example, in *An Essay in Aid of a Grammar of Assent*: 'They come, not so much to lose what they have, as to gain what they have not; and in order that, by means of what they have, more may be given to them.'[8] The idea of the inclusion of all possible

8   For the way that Newman's philosophical viewpoint also stresses the complementarity and mutual dependence of different areas of study within the scientific project, see Laurence Richardson, *Newman's Approach to Knowledge* (Leominster: Gracewing, 2007), especially 144–5. Newman, in *An Essay in Aid of a Grammar of Assent* (Notre Dame, Indiana: University of Notre Dame Press), 302, makes a similar point, on how Christianity builds on what is known by natural means, rather than replacing what is already known: 'Next, as to its relation to nature. As I have said, Christianity is simply an addition to it; it does not supersede or contradict it; it recognises and depends on it, and that of necessity: for how possibly can it prove its claims except by an appeal to what men have already?' For more on how Newman's theory of knowledge is related to Aristotle's phronesis, as well as its relation to the work of other philosophers, including MacIntyre, but also non-Catholic philosophers (such

elements in a developing tradition is emphasized explicitly by Jones, as we shall see. This stress on inclusion lies behind Waugh's and Spark's understanding of the relationship between Britishness and Catholicism, as well.

The theory of how an integrating tradition develops has continued to be elaborated within British Catholic thinking after the time of Jones, Waugh and Spark, especially by the Scottish-born philosopher Alasdair MacIntyre. Famous for advocating an ethics based on an Aristotelian theory of the virtues, another important aspect of his work is the theorization of how intellectual traditions work internally, and interact with each other, and he argues that it is only in the context of a tradition that any kind of understanding is possible. In his famous study *After Virtue*[9] he argued that ethics up to the Renaissance in Western countries developed according to an intelligible tradition, but that this tradition has been lost, with only fragments remaining, which do not add up to a coherent whole. The inability of the inhabitants of contemporary Western countries to engage in rational arguments on ethics with each other, he suggests, is due to the fact that they do not share in any tradition which would make engagement possible. In his study *Three Rival Versions of Moral Enquiry* he argues for the superiority of the (Thomistic) tradition over other ways of understanding how moral enquiry might be conducted (encyclopaedia and genealogy);[10] he also explains here how Aquinas both integrated the Augustinian and Aristotelian traditions, and left the resulting system open to further development, such that the tradition was not closed.[11] MacIntyre highlights

---

as Collingwood, Arendt, Gadamer and Habermas), see Joseph Dunne, *Back to the Rough Ground: 'Phronesis' and 'Techne' in Modern Philosophy and in Aristotle* (Notre Dame, IN: University of Notre Dame Press, 1992). See also Alasdair MacIntyre, 'How Can We Learn What *Veritatis Splendor* Has to Teach?', *The Thomist* 58.2 (1994), 175, for a clear restatement of the principle that Christian Revelation adds to, but does not contradict, what is discoverable by reason from the Natural Law, based on the encyclical *Veritatis Splendor* rather than on Newman's statement.

9   Alasdair MacIntyre, *After Virtue: A Study in Moral Theory* (2nd edn) (London: Duckworth, 1985).
10 Alasdair MacIntyre, *Three Rival Versions of Moral Enquiry: Encyclopaedia, Genealogy, and Tradition* (Notre Dame, IN: University of Notre Dame Press, 1990).
11 Ibid., 124.

the importance of Newman as a theorist of tradition[12] and uses the idea of a cumulative tradition to explain how philosophy (or any other field of intellectual inquiry) develops in terms of a narrative in which earlier stages of understanding are necessary to the development of later stages of fuller understanding, which in turn throw greater light on the earlier stages. He describes this process in an article on the philosophy of science, commenting for example: 'The criterion of a successful theory is that it enables us to understand its predecessors in a newly intelligible way ... It introduces new standards for evaluating the past ... It recasts the narrative which constitutes the continuous reconstruction of the scientific tradition.'[13] So the traditional notion of a developing and cumulative idea, important in Catholic philosophy and prominent in British Catholic thinking, is what allows Jones, Waugh and Spark to achieve a harmonious answer to the question as to whether Britishness and Catholicism can coexist in a single person's identity, despite the acute potential for conflict.

A final chapter will address the work of two other important and well-known British Catholic authors of the twentieth century, G. K. Chesterton and Graham Greene. For both of them, nationality plays a prominent part in their work, but they do not approach the issue of nationality from the harmonizing position identified in the case of Jones, Waugh and Spark. This part of the discussion is designed to show how they differ in their approach from the other three authors, and thus that being a British Catholic writing in the twentieth century does not inevitably lead an author to express the harmonizing theory of identity that is implicit in the work of Jones, Waugh and Spark. In the case of Greene, though his novels often feature

---

[12] In Alasdair MacIntyre, *Whose Justice? Which Rationality?* (Notre Dame, IN: University of Notre Dame Press, 1988), 353–4.

[13] Alasdair MacIntyre, 'Epistemological Crises, Dramatic Narrative, and the Philosophy of Science', *The Tasks of Philosophy: Selected Essays* Vol. 1 (Cambridge: Cambridge University Press, 2006), 11. Canadian Catholic philosopher Charles Taylor also makes important use of the concept of narrative, seeing it as an inescapable part of the moral life, and the form in which selves understand their identity – see Charles Taylor, *Sources of the Self: The Making of Modern Identity* (Cambridge: Cambridge University Press, 1989), especially 47–52.

British expatriate characters who give the impression of being more at home abroad, he does not theorize or explain this tendency in terms connected with the problematics of Britishness and Catholicism, while where the clash between Britishness and Catholicism is thematized, as, for example, in *Brighton Rock*, the question as to how Britishness and Catholicism might be reconciled is not explored. In the case of Chesterton, for whom national identity is a constant theme, his philosophy of nationality is arguably a kind of Romantic philosophy, in which the various national characters are discrete entities, so that issues of miscegenation and reconciling of internal conflicts within identities are not his concern.

Jones', Waugh's and Spark's negotiations with the issue of nationality recognize and highlight divisions and conflicts and do not celebrate unitary national identities. In the following chapters, this study will seek to show that by understanding national identity as emergent rather than given, and supported by the theory of the developing and integrative tradition available to them from Catholic thinking, Jones, Waugh and Spark are all able to conceive of each individual as achieving an identity which can unify diverse, even superficially conflicting, national and cultural elements as part of a coherent journey; this journey's destination is understood as spiritual, while its history includes a diversity of material and spiritual components.

CHAPTER I

David Jones: Sacramentality and National History

A concern with issues of national identity, national history and tradition saturates David Jones' work and is prominent in almost everything he wrote. His concerns about national identity, however, form part of a wider theory, which includes an understanding of the nature of art, within a vision of an overarching religious frame for all culture. It is thus not possible totally to separate the theoretical elements of his understanding of national identity from his view of the arts and theology. This chapter is intended to show how these concerns fit together and reinforce each other in his works.

Jones is now better known to many for his visual artwork than for his writing, and his writing might be said to have been neglected, despite its high valuation by prominent poets of his time, such as T. S. Eliot, Auden and Yeats.[1] His writing can be divided into his poetic work and his essays (as well as his letters), and this chapter will trace some key themes relating to his understanding of nationality as he explains them in his essays, before examining the way these themes emerge in three of his major volumes of poetic work. As the circumstances of his early life had a significant impact on his later concerns, the discussion will start by taking note of important biographical details which have a bearing on his attitudes and the development of his theory, particularly on his understanding of national identity.

---

1   See Foreword by W. S. Mervyn to David Jones, *In Parenthesis* (New York: New York Review of Books, 2003) (*IP*), i. Further references to this edition are given after quotations in the text. For a discussion of the neglect of Jones' poetic work see Elizabeth Judge, 'Notes on the Outside: David Jones, Unshared Backgrounds and (the Absence of) Canonicity', *Essays in Literary History* 68.1 (Spring 2001), 179–213.

Biography

David Jones was born in 1895, in Brockley, Kent, a town now absorbed into the suburbs of south-east London.[2] His father, James Jones, was Welsh, from north-east Wales, but had settled in London, working in printing, and his mother, Alice Bradshaw, was English, daughter of Ebenezer Bradshaw, a 'mast- and block-maker', and scion of a London-area shipbuilding family from Rotherhithe, by the Thames, although there was some Italian element on her mother's side (*Dai G*, 19). Both sides of his family history were important to him and helped to shape his poetry, but the Welsh side had a particularly strong imaginative impact, and has led to controversy among later commentators.

Jones makes a very clear statement of his attitude to his Welshness, and how it began, in an autobiographical essay, 'In Illo Tempore': 'From about the age of six, I felt I belonged to my father's people and their land, though brought up in an entirely English atmosphere.'[3] He made holiday visits to Wales as a child,[4] but did not live in Wales until adulthood, after his return from the First World War, and then only for a short period, spending time at the artists' settlement at Capel-y-Ffin in the Black Mountains, near the border with England, and on Caldey Island, with the Benedictine monks, on and off from 1924 to 1927 (*Dai G*, 31–44). Early in the First World War he joined a Welsh regiment, the Royal Welsh Fusiliers (*Dai G*, 20). His father, apart from singing to him in Welsh, did not attempt to teach him Welsh, and was in fact not strong in the language himself (*Dai G*, 20, *The DG*, 31); Jones' subsequent attempts to learn the language foundered on

---

2   David Jones, *Dai Greatcoat: A Self-Portrait of David Jones in his Letters*, René Hague, ed. (London: Faber, 2008) (*Dai G*), 20. Further references to this edition are given after quotations in the text.
3   David Jones, *The Dying Gaul and Other Writings*, Harman Grisewood, ed. (London: Faber, 1978) (*The DG*), 23. Further references to this edition are given after quotations in the text.
4   Ibid., 23 and David Jones, *Epoch and Artist*, Harman Grisewood, ed. (London: Faber, 1959) (*EA*), 27. Further references to this edition are given after quotations in the text.

the grammar, though he clearly built up a familiarity with a wide range of vocabulary. The discrepancy between his feeling of attachment to Wales and the limited time he spent there is noted, for example, by his friend, René Hague, editor of the published volume of his letters, *Dai Greatcoat*. Hague blames his fascination with all things Welsh, together with his inability to learn Welsh, for 'the most serious blemishes in his poetry', because of 'His ingenuous use of Welsh words as though they had some magical quality...' (Hague in *Dai G*, 24). This criticism is arguably however to miss the point, as Hague almost admits in the same paragraph, when he says that Jones viewed Welshness as a universal (Hague in *Dai G*, 23), that is, a universal quality in the philosophical sense.[5] Jones' understanding of sacramentality in art means that Welsh words, and in fact any words, do have something like magical qualities, which bring to the mind of the reader cultural deposits that can in no other way be animated.

Jones started to attend art school at the early age of fourteen, first at Camberwell School of Art. His artistic education was interrupted by the First World War but resumed afterwards at the Westminster School of Art from 1919 to 1921 (*Dai G*, 20, 28). After this, during the 1920s, he spent much of his time with the group of Catholic artists led by the sculptor Eric Gill – this group moved from Ditchling Common in Sussex to Capel-y-Ffin in Wales, then to North Dean, Buckinghamshire, and formed a guild (which Jones did not join formally), influenced by ideas such as the neo-Thomism of Jacques Maritain and Gill's own anti-industrialism (*Dai G*, 30–1).[6] Jones continued to be a painter, engraver and calligrapher

---

5   Staudt, *At the Turn of a Civilization*, 16, argues that Jones' Wales and Yeats' Byzantium are 'alternate worlds ruled by the poetic imagination', although Jones' Wales, unlike Yeats' Byzantium, is connected to the real place.

6   For the influence of Maritain on Jones see Thomas Dilworth, 'David Jones and the Maritain Conversation', in *David Jones: Diversity in Unity: Studies in his Literary and Visual Art*, Belinda Humphrey and Anne Price-Owen, eds (Cardiff: University of Wales Press, 2000); Aidan Nichols, *Redeeming Beauty: Soundings in Sacral Aesthetics* (Aldershot: Ashgate, 2007), 125–42; and Rowan Williams (who discusses how Jones' aesthetic thinking incorporates and surpasses that of Maritain), *Grace and Necessity: Reflections on Art and Love* (London: Continuum, 2005), 62–89.

throughout his writing career, and his sacramental theory of art is a key component of his essayistic work, as well as influencing his poetry, and interacting with his understanding of nationality.

A further important biographical event which helped to shape Jones' theories and poetry was his conversion to Catholicism, which took place in 1921 (*Dai G*, 21), his interest dating from his First World War years (*EA*, 28). He saw the Catholic liturgy for the first time near the front line (*Dai G*, 248–9), although he recalls having had instincts towards the sacramental as a child, despite the low-church Protestant atmosphere of his family: he recounts carrying a cross he made himself round the garden of his house on a Good Friday, when about seven years old (*Dai G*, 246–7). As well as leading to his introduction to a circle of Catholic artists and writers, Jones' conversion is connected to his deep concern with the sacramental principle, which provided the foundation for his theory of art. Jones as a Catholic also develops the fascination with the Middle Ages common in British Catholic writers, and in his case especially with the Welsh Middle Ages, in particular, the transitional period from the end of the Roman Empire, through the arrival of the Anglo-Saxons in Britain, up to the thirteenth century and the last independent Welsh prince, Llywelyn.

David Jones' Essays

David Jones' published essays are contained in two volumes, *Epoch and Artist*, published in 1959, and *The Dying Gaul*, published posthumously in 1978. Much of the writing contained in these volumes concerns Welsh-related themes, and there are also some important statements of his theory of art. This section of the study will highlight some of the topics that run through his pieces on Welsh and British history, identity and legends, and will also bring out aspects of his theory of art with a view to demonstrating how his sacramental theory plays a part in the presentation of nationality in his poetry.

In his writings Jones talks comparatively little about his own experiences of Wales. Apart from mentioning his stays during the 1920s at Capel-y-Ffin and Caldey Island, he also recalls his first trip to Wales, as a child, which was accompanied by a sense of crossing a border, and a meeting with his grandfather at St Trillo's chapel on the north coast (*EA*, 27); he mentions spending time painting in the Teifi Valley 'in the summer before 1914' (*EA*, 28), and finding himself training in Llandudno after signing up with the Royal Welsh Fusiliers early in the First World War (*EA*, 28). However these are passing references on which he does not dwell. He does express concern for the survival of traditional Welsh culture in Wales, especially the language, in a number of letters reproduced in the volumes of essays ('Welshness in Wales', *EA*, 51–3; 'Welsh Wales', *EA*, 53–4; 'Welsh Culture', *The DG*, 117–22) and in the talk 'A London Artist Looks at Contemporary Wales' (*The DG*, 35–40) – in this talk he is particularly anxious on account of a proposed scheme to industrialize Anglesey and populate it from the English Midlands, and explains the importance of the language and of geographical associations to the survival of Welsh historical memory. He also expresses regret for his own limited competence in Welsh, especially in the essay 'On the Difficulties of One Writer of Welsh Affinity Whose Language is English' (*The DG*, 30–4), where he also discusses a more general lack of shared cultural terrain that can be assumed between poets working in the twentieth century and their readers. However, while the task of the contemporary artist, together with the difficulties of the artist in a mechanical age, is a crucial area of concern to him, his interest in Wales does not focus on the contemporary situation, and his promotion of the cultural memory of Wales is not only intended for the benefit of his Welsh contemporaries.

David Jones, not unusually for a Catholic writer, pays a special attention to the Middle Ages. Given this affinity to medieval Wales, he is disposed to concentrate on the period from the beginnings of the formation of Welsh identity at the end of the Roman Empire's presence in Britain, from around the fourth century, to the end of the line of independent Welsh princes with the death of Llywelyn ap Gruffydd in 1282. He became particularly absorbed in the 'sub-Roman' period, and was keen to show how the dynasty of the Welsh princes was descended directly from the last

Roman rulers, and how Welsh cultural traditions included an awareness of this continuity, as well as various signs and tales alluding to it.[7] This subject is recurrent in Jones' writing, forming part of many of his essays, and is the central concern of, for example, 'The Heritage of Early Britain' (*EA*, 196–201), and 'The Welsh Dragon' (*The DG*, 108–16), which traces the origin of the contemporary Welsh flag to a Roman battle standard.

The presence of the names of such figures as Cunedda Wledig in Welsh legend, a Roman war leader who is at the root of the dynasty of the Gwynedd princes, makes Welsh culture unique in the island of Britain, as Jones is frequently at pains to point out, since it is the only repository of a tradition continuous with the island's Roman history still to be found in Britain. Therefore the Welsh cultural tradition is an important part of the cultural tradition of all those who inhabit those parts of Britain which belonged to the Roman Empire, that is, everywhere south of the Antonine Wall, and is not only of relevance to the Welsh. All these points emerge strongly in the talk 'Wales and the Crown' (*EA*, 39–48), where, as well as referring to Cunedda, and to other Roman officials of the time who left their names as the basis of the names of Welsh regions, Romanus for Rhufoniog and Marianus for Meirionnydd (*EA*, 41), he suggests that the Welsh during the times of the princes were unable to unite under a supreme ruler, and were susceptible to accepting the authority of a monarch based in London, because their own dynasties were descended from subordinate Roman rulers, and a tradition of the unity of the whole island is present in their legendary deposits (*EA*, 45). London derives prestige from its mythic associations with the god Nodens (Llud in Welsh, Lud in English), and from the tradition of the head of mythical figure Brân being buried under the White Mount, in London, to protect the island (*EA*, 44–5). Another unifying factor he emphasizes is that Cunedda and his companions moved to North Wales from 'north of the Wall' (*EA*, 42) – their association with areas now in Scotland brings all three modern nations of the island into the account. Importantly, he does not forget to mention in passing that

---

7   David Blamires, 'Roma Aurea Roma in the Writings of David Jones', *Anglo-Welsh Review* 22.50 (Autumn 1973), discusses Rome as it features across Jones' writings.

Cunedda's 'religion was probably the official one, Christianity' (*EA*, 41). Thus the Welsh tradition forms a link in a continuous chain of tradition, and constitutes the only connecting link, between the Coronation of Queen Elizabeth, which he is writing about in this piece, and the Roman Empire in Britain: the current monarchy can claim continuity with Roman authority, but only by acknowledging the Welsh tradition.

Apart from this unifying potential of the Welsh tradition for the whole island, a potential alternative unifying narrative to the later Protestant British narrative of union, Jones' interest in the days of the dissolution of the Roman Empire also takes on significance for him in terms of patterns of world history. Like Evelyn Waugh in *Helena*, David Jones sees a connection between the era of the collapse of the Roman Empire and the twentieth-century era he is living in, which he also considers to be a period of civilizational collapse. He is influenced in this by the theories of Oswald Spengler, as he frequently admits himself (for example, *EA*, 205, 242). In the talk 'The Viae: The Roman Roads in Britain' (*EA*, 189–95) he imagines the inhabitants of late Roman and early post-Roman Britain watching the road network built by the Romans fall into gradual and partial disuse. He makes the parallel with the twentieth century explicit: 'Those of us who have lived through the whole, or even part, of the first half of the twentieth century understand, or should understand, the end of the world brings radical but by no means uniform change' (*EA*, 191). The Roman roads represent the technical and bureaucratic civilization of Rome, which was superseded by the less technical medieval civilization. However, importantly for Jones, the collapse of classical Rome made way for Christian civilization, in Britain and in Europe generally. He concludes the talk by mentioning the Helen of the legend of The Dream of Macsen Wledig: in this legend Helen, the wife of Macsen Wledig (based on the historical figure Magnus Maximus, a late-Roman general active in Britain, and usurper of the Western Empire), causes roads to be built for the defence of the island. Although this is a different legendary figure from Helena, mother of Constantine (of Waugh's novel), he suggests that some conflation of the two, and possibly an earlier Celtic Elen figure, must account for the power of the legendary figure Helen of the Armies, after whom a Roman road in Wales, Sarn Elen, is still named (*EA*, 195).

Among the components of Jones' vision of the cultural inheritance of late Roman and early post-Roman Britain, the Arthur legend plays a prominent part. The essays 'The Arthurian Legend' (*EA*, 202–11) and 'The Myth of Arthur' (*EA*, 212–59) are dedicated to the theme, but it is a staple element in his work more generally. He draws attention, in 'The Arthurian Legend', to the fact that Arthur could have been a historical figure and, if so, would have been a post-Roman cavalry leader, fighting the incoming Angles and Saxons, leading a band similar to the one described in the early Welsh poem the *Gododdin* (*EA*, 206–7). One way in which the legend is important is that it is the only well-known legend to form part of both the Welsh and English traditions, even if it takes different forms in each, as he points out in 'The Myth of Arthur' (*EA*, 216).[8] Another way in which it is significant for Jones, and connects with wider themes, is addressed in 'The Dying Gaul' (*The DG*, 50–8). This essay is not principally about Arthur, but explores the way that defeat appears to be important in Celtic legend: the essay begins with a discussion of the famous classical statue of a dying Gaul, a cast of which Jones used to draw at art school. The point about this culture of defeat is that each defeat brings with it a victory on another level: '... the Dying Gaul is not dead yet' (*The DG*, 58). Here he proclaims that Celtic identity continues to live in art, through features such as the presence of complex formal patterns and an attachment to specific places and times (which he sees as Celtic qualities), exemplified in the work of James Joyce (*The DG*, 58). The essay 'Welsh Poetry' (*EA*, 56–65) makes a similar artistic point, reminding the reader of the influence of Welsh metre on Gerard Manley Hopkins, and of his influence on subsequent poetry in English: thus the marginalization of the Welsh language has not put an end to its influence (*EA*, 64).[9] However, there is a hint at another kind of victory in defeat: in describing in detail the band of warriors represented in Aneirin's sixth-century poem the *Gododdin*, who ride from the north, possibly from what is now Edinburgh, to fight the Angles at Catraeth, a loca-

---

8   See also David Blamires, *David Jones: Artist and Writer* (Manchester: Manchester University Press, 1971), 178, for this point.
9   He makes the claim for Welsh influence on Hopkins and also on the English Metaphysical poets, in 'Welsh Culture', *The DG*, 121.

tion in what is now Yorkshire, and are heavily defeated, Jones recounts that they are represented as having had recourse to the Sacrament of Penance before battle: therefore they are Christian, unlike the Angles (*EA*, 58–9). Though Jones does not make the point explicitly here, what is implied is that it is their Christianity which is victorious in Britain, despite their defeat, not the Angles' paganism – victorious by means other than war, however. He comes closer to being explicit in 'The Myth of Arthur': the political and military loss of the island by the Romano-Britons occurs at the same time as an enthusiastic and expansive outward movement of Celtic Christianity (*EA*, 253–4).

In his short essay on English art, 'An Aspect of the Art of England' (*The DG*, 59–62), Jones points to a pied, mottled quality as being an identifying characteristic of English art, making the obvious connection with Hopkins,[10] but also connecting the idea with an old Greek name for Britain, the 'Pretanic Isles', which he understands as meaning speckled, and links with the Romans' term 'Picts' (*The DG*, 59); in addition he regards the complex geology of the island as contributing to this quality. He places English culture firmly within European culture: 'As the whole of our culture, lock, stock and barrel, is but a part of West European culture and has, historically and at each turn, taken its cue from continental developments (I speak of main trends and not in detail), it follows that our native genius has had to express itself within those developments' (*The DG*, 60). A longer essay, 'Wales and Visual Form' (*The DG*, 63–93) considers the lack of visual art surviving from past periods of Welsh history, and explains it as the result of Wales being a highland zone, with a corresponding limitation to its development in terms of material culture compared with its corresponding lowland zone, England, while Wales, in compensation, excelled in verbal art.

Jones' theory of art and sacrament is the most distinctive part of his thinking and shapes his views on other areas. He himself links his sacramental theory with his approach to nationality in the 'Preface by the Author' to *Epoch and Artist*. Having explained that the contemporary stage of

---

10 See Philip Pacey, *David Jones and Other Wonder Voyagers: Essays by Philip Pacey* (Bridgend: Poetry Wales Press, 1982), 45, for the connection between Hopkins and Jones, through their sense of the particular.

civilization tends to a belief that 'particular facts are no more than they are', a view which, he claims, threatens understanding of the 'Welsh *res*', as well as of 'what is said to be done at the altar', and artists' activity, he goes on:

> Hence, what in this collection touches upon the historic deposits of Wales and of the Island of Britain is, in the eye of my mind, seen as all of a piece with the question of sign and sacrament and so with what I do when I set about a work, be it a water-colour drawing or *The Anathemata*. The problems and dilemmas at least *feel* all one to me. (*EA*, 17)

Jones' theory of art and sacrament, which he explains in detail in essays such as 'Art and Democracy' (*EA*, 85–96), 'Religion and the Muses' (*EA*, 97–106), 'Art and Sacrament' (*EA*, 143–79), 'The Utile' (*EA*, 180–5), 'Art in Relation to War' (*The DG*, 123–66), and 'Use and Sign' (*The DG*, 177–85), as well as referring to it repeatedly elsewhere, is based on the Catholic both-and attitude to the material and the spiritual, that is, both are real and both are good, and they are interlinked. Man is the only creature participating in both the spiritual and material realms (unlike material animals and spiritual angels), and is thereby, Jones concludes, by nature, the sign-making creature, or the artist (as he explains in 'Art and Sacrament', *EA*, 148–50). Therefore humans must act in a sign-making way, or be frustrated (as he emphasizes, for example, in 'Art in Relation to War' (*The DG*, 163).

An important element of Jones' theory is that a sign does not just represent, but re-presents: that is, an art work, for example, is a reality, not only a link to something not present. He elaborates this position more than once, but a thorough exposition is to be found in 'Art and Sacrament' (*EA*, 170–5),[11] where he uses Hogarth's painting *The Shrimp Girl* as an example, arguing that the painting makes real the idea Hogarth had when making the painting. He also imagines an artist saying to himself, 'This is not a representation of a mountain, it *is* "mountain" under the form of paint' (*EA*, 170). He credits Post-Impressionist theory, encountered by him in art school in 1919, as the source of the idea for him, recounting how he also started at this time to associate the idea with the sacramental significance of the Eucharist in Christianity (*EA*, 171). There is a relationship, or analogy,

---

11   See Williams, *Grace and Necessity*, 85–9, for an important analysis of this essay.

between this strong version of the way that a work of art shows forth, and is, what it represents, and the specifically Catholic understanding of the Eucharist as a re-enactment of the Crucifixion, the main event having happened once historically and geographically, but the effects of which can be called forth, not only remembered, every time the Eucharist is celebrated – Jones acknowledges this relationship in the same essay (*EA*, 162–3, 163 note 1, 167–8), while claiming that all Christians are committed to some version of sign-making. Elsewhere, he insists that all human life is committed to, and impossible without, sign-making, whether acknowledged as such or not (as he argues, for example, in 'Use and Sign', *The DG*, 182–4).

In 'A Christmas Message 1961' (*The DG*, 167–76) Jones makes many of the above points on art and sacrament, but addresses them to a Catholic audience, and emphasizes such theological insights as the analogy between the Incarnation and the Eucharist (*The DG*, 171), that is, that the sacramental nature of the Eucharist – the principle of spiritual realities operating through material signs, and the signs being what they represent – is made possible by Jesus being God and man. He also, at the beginning of this essay, connects Catholic thinking with a commitment to specific times and places: 'In contrast with some beliefs the belief of Catholic Church commits its adherents, in a most inescapable manner, to the body and the embodied; hence to history, to locality, to epoch and site, to sense-perception, to the contactual, the known, the felt, the seen, the handled, the cared for, the tended, the conserved; to the qualitative and to the intimate'. (*The DG*, 167) Thus there is a chain of reasoning in Jones' thought, which connects the Catholic belief in the material and the spiritual, and in art and sacrament, to the importance of specific, experienced, time and place; this sacramental attitude should not lead to a cultivation of the 'unembodied concept' (*The DG*, 167), but rather 'things of all sorts' are to be 'raised above the utile to the status of *signa*' (*The DG*, 167) – and the *material* of a religious sacrament is a *signum*, as is a work of art. The consequence of this theory for nationality is that national cultural traditions, legends and 'deposits' (as Jones frequently describes them)[12] are part of the *signa* that artists raise

---

12 Stuart Piggott, 'David Jones and the Past of Man', in *Agenda: An Anthology: The First Four Decades (1959–1993)*, William Cookson, ed. (Manchester: Carcanet, 1996), 333, remarks on how 'deposits' is an important word for Jones.

up, part of the reality of the works of art in which they appear, and partake of a kind of sacramental significance. On the other hand, as we shall see in connection to Jones' poetry, while the poet can only use the deposits related to the locality the poet knows, more than one layer of national deposits may be attached to a particular locality, and those layers of different traditions are then in no way incompatible, but part of a kind of artistic archaeology of the place. In his essay 'James Joyce's Dublin' (*EA*, 303–7), Jones credits Joyce with having achieved what an artist should achieve, that is, 'to make the universal shine out from the particular' (*EA*, 304), and he also makes the argument, important to his poems, that the West is a fusion of Celtic, Latin and Germanic identities, all of which Joyce brings out through the particularity of early twentieth-century Dublin (*EA*, 304–5).

Jones was haunted by a sense that the civilizational conditions of his time tended to militate against artistic-sacramental activity, which is nevertheless necessary for natural (as opposed to supernatural) human fulfilment. He frequently referred to Spengler in connection with his sense that the twentieth century was an era of civilizational collapse, but Jones' worry is specifically the idea that what he sees as a technocracy is hostile to sign-making, and that individuals are discouraged from thinking or acting artistically (for example, in 'Notes on the 1930s', *The DG*, 41–9, especially 44–5). The work of those who nevertheless continue to produce art works is also made all the more difficult by the fact that potential readers are less likely to share the knowledge of a body of historical allusions with the artist, an obstacle to the artist producing a 'valid' work of art, that is, a work of art which shows forth its own time, and its own time's relation to that time's history (for example, in 'On the Difficulties of One Writer of Welsh Affinity Whose Language is English', *The DG*, especially 34). Jones struggled with this difficulty in his poetic work, trying to make the traditions of the island, including the Welsh traditions, valid and effective for the twentieth-century British reader, but never confident that he was achieving this.[13]

---

13   A. M. Allchin, 'On Not Knowing Welsh: David Jones and the Matter of Wales', in *David Jones: Diversity in Unity: Studies in his Literary and Visual Art*, Belinda

In Parenthesis

In Parenthesis is Jones' earliest writing, published in 1937. It contains a mixture of prose and verse, and describes his experiences in the First World War (he appears in the persona of Private John Ball), accompanied by copious literary and historical allusions.[14] Very striking is the close attention to the physical details and sensations of the experience, in parallel with the rich background of historical, literary and cultural association. Jones, as always, provides an explanatory preface (also included in *EA*, 32–8) and specifies that he is writing about the period from 'early in December 1915' to 'early in July 1916' (*IP*, ix). He notes that the War became more mechanized after this early period (*IP*, ix), a development which, given his misgivings about the sign-making potential of mechanical contrivances (which he details later in the preface, *IP*, xiv), may explain why he chooses to focus on this early period, even though he was present during the later period as well. He explains that with him in his regiment were mainly Londoners, together with some from Wales, a mixture he describes as 'representative': 'Together they bore in their bodies the genuine tradition of the Island of Britain, from Bendigeid Vran to Jingle and Marie Lloyd. These were the children of Doll Tearsheet. Those are before Caractacus was' (*IP*, x). So he is indicating a common geographical denominator, Caractacus and Bendigeid Vran being figures in Welsh historical and legendary memory dating back to times when the Brythonic forebears of the Welsh occupied most of Britain, not only Wales; but at the same time he is emphasizing the newness and contemporaneity of the London culture of those in the regiment, in contrast to the reach towards ancient origins of the Welsh folklore. He goes on to name similarities of temperament between the

---

Humphrey and Anne Price-Owen, eds (Cardiff: University of Wales Press, 2000), 80, notes that Jones was concerned that technological civilization would make conditions unfavourable for art and Welsh tradition.

14 For a detailed account of Jones' experiences as a soldier in the First World War see Thomas Dilworth, *David Jones in the Great War* (London: Enitharmion Press, 2012).

two groups, while yet insisting on their difference: 'Both speak in parables, the wit of both is quick, both are natural poets; yet no two groups could well be more dissimilar' (*IP*, x). He does not further define the differences in the preface; rather he addresses the issue of the way he links together present experience with cultural echoes: 'I suppose at no time did one so much live with a consciousness of the past, the very remote, and the more immediate and trivial past, both superficially and more subtly' (*IP*, xi). He lists some of the associations which he was led to make at the time, and which feature in the body of the poem, including history of the classical world, ancient and modern British history, English folk songs and Celtic mythology. These are the kind of elements which Jones saw as layers in the British cultural deposit: in connection with the Celtic mythology he makes its geographical reach clearer, writing that it 'lies, a subterranean influence as a deep water troubling, under every tump of this Island, like Merlin complaining under his deep rock' (*IP*, xi). So he asserts the presence of the Welsh-Celtic associations over Britain as a whole, denying that they are only Welsh.

Jones, sensitive to the possible criticism that the strong Welsh element in the poem will only be relevant to Welsh readers, takes on this potential objection again in a later paragraph of the preface:

> Ladely Worm, Brunanburh, Fair Worcester City, Fair Maid of Kent: these, rightly, for our ears, discover a whole English complex; whereas the Boar Trwyth, Badon Hill, Troy Novaunt, Elen of the Hosts, will only find response in those who, by blood or inclination, feel a kinship with the more venerable culture in that hotch-potch which is ourselves. Yet that elder element is integral to our tradition. From Layamon to Blake 'Sabrina' would call up spirits rather than 'Ypwinesfloet'. (*IP*, xiii)

It may be that the names Jones cites as evoking an English tradition will be obscure to many an English reader, but the argument here is that names coming from the Welsh-Celtic tradition underlie English culture and participate in it. In fact they have even on occasion substituted for Germanic elements which the first English will have brought with them from the continent: for example, the Celtic nymph or divinity associated with the River Severn, Sabrina or Hafren, figures in English literature as a sorcerer figure, and no Germanic figure does. Thus English culture, although generally with less long a memory than its Welsh counterpart, has to some extent co-opted the Welsh-British element where ancient mythology is concerned, thus connecting itself with the early history and prehistory of the island in a way in which its largely forgotten Germanic traditions could not. He then goes further in the same direction, citing Christopher Dawson, who is referring to R. G. Collingwood, in order to introduce the idea that there is a tradition of siding with lost causes in western Britain, which has become typical in Britain as a whole, a notion which explains Arthur being the favourite heroic figure of the English Middle Ages: this idea, as well as reinforcing Jones' argument about the adoption of Celtic-Welsh motifs into English mythology, and their displacing of the Germanic motifs that might otherwise have been dominant, also provides a link to Jones' recurrent theme of the Celtic legend of defeat which nevertheless represents survival and victory at a spiritual level.

In Parenthesis is divided into seven 'Parts', each presenting a different stage of the main character's (John Ball's) war experience. He starts in a training camp in southern England, embarks for France, and arrives at the French port, in Part 1. Part 2 begins in a camp away from the front line in Northern France, and describes a march towards it, with Part 3 completing the march to the front line, and portraying the entry into and installation in the trenches. Part 4 is an extended representation of life in the section of trenches they have entered in Part 3, a section which is presented as being in a northern, flat and watery part of the Front. Part 5 sees Ball and his companions at a recuperation and training camp behind the lines, but then making the march south to the chalky downs of the Somme area. The build-up to the assault on Mametz Wood, in which Ball is involved, takes place in Part 6, then comes the assault itself, with Ball's injury, in Part 7. All these events closely follow Jones' own experiences.

From the point of view of Jones' expression of his understanding of British identity in the work, it is not so much the events which are important as the linguistic and cultural web in which the experiences take shape. Until the assault on Mametz Wood in the final Part there is arguably no story-line, and few events, apart from moving from one place to another. Jones includes in the soldiers' language a large amount of military slang and technical language, much of it specific to the trench warfare of the First

World War and thus connecting the people and events portrayed firmly to a given time and place. He also includes contemporary London and Welsh popular culture, in order to particularize the origins of the men around him geographically: he uses cockney slang, references to contemporary places in London, and popular songs, such as the Welsh folk and rugby song, 'Sospan Fach' (*IP*, 53, 201 note 44). This establishing of the time and place of John Ball and the people round him is deepened by cultural allusions which build up their historical inheritance. The Welsh-related heritage is prominent, and this comes in the form of *Y Gododdin*, the sixth-century poem attributed to Aneirin, quotations from which preface each section.[15] Works from medieval Welsh manuscripts, such as the Welsh legends conventionally collected as *The Mabinogion*, including, for example, *Culhwch ac Olwen*, an early Arthurian story, are also important, together with the poems known as the *Englynion y Beddau*, and the stories and fragments known as the *Triads*. Jones includes these poems and stories in order to actualize elements of the Middle Ages, but also because they contain roots in earlier Celtic cultures. Malory is present as an important way of introducing the Arthur legend,[16] and thus represents an English-Welsh fusion, as does Gerard Manley Hopkins, who is a source for the title of Part 5 ('Squat Garlands for White Knights', *IP*, 100; see also 213 note 1). Shakespeare's *Henry V* features heavily, strengthening the English cultural element, and recalling the idea of British people fighting in France, but it also tacitly supports the idea of an English-Welsh coming together, given the prominent part played by the Welsh at the Battle of Agincourt, and their representation in the play.

Some non-British elements also play a part. In terms of references to the contemporary circumstances, there is the occasional appearance of German, as when the words of the first two lines of the Christmas carol *Es ist ein Ros' entsprungen* are quoted, because John Ball can hear them

---

15 For more on *Y Gododdin* in *In Parenthesis*, see Paul Robichaud, *Making the Past Present: David Jones, the Middle Ages, and Modernity* (Washington, DC: Catholic University of America Press, 2007), 55–69.

16 See Robichaud, *Making the Past Present*, 15–25, for Malory's influence on Jones.

coming from the opposing line (*IP*, 67). Making the connection with the past, Scandinavian mythology and sagas are included in the allusions, as is Irish legend; and, prominently, and as the major French element, the *Song of Roland* is a recurrent source of allusions, although Jones does not quote in the original language in the main text. The culture of the Latin and Greek classical world is included through the theme of Troy. In addition there are allusions to the Bible and to the Latin liturgy of the Catholic Church, and the work ends with a series of six biblical quotations, in Latin and English (*IP*, 226), which come after the footnotes, a position which highlights the fact that the footnotes are an integral part of the work. The choice of sources for his allusions embodies Jones' two frequently asserted contentions: that Welsh culture underlies English culture, such that English culture cannot be understood without a Welsh perspective being included; and that British culture as a whole is part of, and inseparable from, a larger Western European unity, formed from a mingling of Celtic, Latin and German elements, and given a spiritual form by Christianity.

A significant episode of Welsh cultural contextualization comes in Part 4, when a Welsh soldier utters the 'boast' (*IP*, 79–84), an invocation of places and events in the past at which the ancestors or forebears of the boast's utterer have been present, which is proclaimed as if the boaster himself had been there. The idea of the boast, as Jones explains in his extensive notes on the passage (*IP*, 207–10 note 37), is inspired by those of the early Welsh poet Taliesin,[17] by the Welsh Arthur's porter Glewlwyd in *Culhwch ac Olwen*, and the Old English boast in the poem *Widsith*. Part of Jones' Welsh soldier's boast is to claim that he has been present at various historical battles, and a prominent element of this claim is associated with having been a member of the Roman legions: 'I am the Loricated Legions' (*IP*, 80). While in the legions he has seen the evacuation of large parts of the legions from Britain during the late Roman period to take part in wars on the continent, leaving the island prone to migration from the outside (*IP*,

---

17 The Welsh-language writer Saunders Lewis noted the strong connection between Taliesin and *In Parenthesis*. See 'A Note', in *Agenda: An Anthology*, William Cookson, ed., 336.

82), and he was also a member of the legion present in Jerusalem at the Crucifixion (*IP*, 83, 210 note 37 L) – the idea of legionaries who had been in, or were from Britain, participating in the events of the New Testament was important to Jones in later poems. Welsh legendary figures of significance to the whole island, such as Helen of the Hosts (Elen Luyddog), Bran the Blessed (both described above) and Arthur ('The War Duke/The Director of Toil', *IP*, 82), are also included in the boast. The boast's function, as well as to highlight the themes of the Welsh heritage of the whole island of Britain, and the inseparability of the Welsh and Roman strands of the island's heritage, is to emphasize that Welsh culture exhibits a longer memory than English – and thus that the English may discover more about the heritage of Britain by consulting Welsh tradition. The idea of the longer memory of Welsh culture recurs in Part 4 when Lance-Corporal Aneirin Lewis, observing efforts to drain the water-logged trenches, is reminded of the Welsh legend of the lost region, Cantref y Gwaelod, which was flooded by the sea because of a forgetful steward. He regrets that another Welshman, Watcyn, does not have the expected awareness of Welsh legend: 'he might have been an Englishman when it came to matters near to Aneirin's heart' (*IP*, 89). Earlier, in Part 1, the same Aneirin Lewis is said to have 'in his Welsh depths a remembrance of the nature of man, of how a lance-corporal's stripe is but held vicariously and from on high, is of one texture with an eternal economy. He brings a manner, baptism, and metaphysical order to the bankruptcy of the occasion [a parade]' (*IP*, 1–2). Corporal Quilter, not obviously Welsh, by contrast, 'knew nothing of these things' (*IP*, 2). Here it seems to be implied that there is not only a deeper memory among at least some of the Welsh soldiers than the average English one, but also a greater understanding of the metaphysical economy of the sign, that understanding to which Jones feared modern technical civilization is inimical.

As we have seen, among the many themes of *In Parenthesis*, the theme of nationality concentrates on the historical shape of national cultures, and their formation through layers of local associations, both historical and legendary, building up from the remote past to the present, and investing physical things, people and places with significance beyond themselves. In addition, in terms of the men of John Ball's regiment, Jones portrays Welsh and English culture as contrasting, in that Welsh culture looks further back and conserves a stronger sacramental, or sign-making, sign-understanding sense. On the other hand he also presents the intertwining and interpenetration of the two cultures, and especially emphasizes the fact that English culture is unthinkable without its underlying Welsh-Brythonic elements. Jones also, remarkably given the First World War context, emphasizes a unity in all Western European culture, founded on the mingling and fusion of Latin, Germanic and Celtic peoples, and with a shared historical foundation in the Roman Empire and a common religious foundation in the Christian (especially Catholic) Church. All these ideas are developed and explored further in his later poetry, and are even more central to his next major written work, *The Anathemata*, than to *In Parenthesis*, where they are perhaps overshadowed by the themes of war and redemption in the midst of catastrophe.

The Anathemata

The Anathemata[18] is a kind of epic poem[19] which explores the historical and legendary foundations of British culture, emphasizing what Jones saw as the foundational period, the late antique, early medieval period, though not confining itself to any one period. Jones imagines a sea voyage from the antique Mediterranean world to the Port of London. This journey forms a skeleton story on which the poem is hung, although only five of the eight sections show parts of the voyage or the stay in London, whereas, of the remaining three, the first section provides prehistorical and geological background to the rest of the poem, while the first and the last two sections together provide a liturgical frame, placing the cultural edifice in a

---

18   David Jones, *The Anathemata: Fragments of an Attempted Writing* (London: Faber, 1972) (*TA*). Further references to this edition are given after quotations in the text.
19   Both Blamires, *David Jones: Artist and Writer*, 205, and Dilworth, *The Shape of Meaning*, 153, compare *The Anathemata* with the *Aeneid*.

supernatural context. The poem is highly allusive, even more densely so than *In Parenthesis*, and is difficult for the reader, as it has, like *In Parenthesis*, little that could be described as a plot, while, unlike *In Parenthesis*, the time, place and action are at times difficult to discern. In the first, seventh and eighth sections, it is often hard to say that anything is 'happening', other than the poet's chain of thoughts.

As he does for *In Parenthesis*, Jones provides a lengthy preface (which also appears in *EA*, 107–37). This contains guidance as to how to read the poem, as well as some useful statements about Jones' attitude to his own national identity, and the notion of national culture which informs *The Anathemata*. He begins by quoting from the prologues to the early medieval *Historia Brittonum*, attributed to the Welsh monk Nennius, in which Nennius, if he is the writer, speaks of drawing together the materials he can find, including histories of the Britons, Roman histories, works by Church Fathers and histories of the 'Scots and Saxons' (*TA*, 9). Jones' procedure, like Nennius', is to gather together sources of Celtic, Roman, Germanic and ecclesiastical origins, although for a poem, not a history. He goes on to identify what *The Anathemata* is about:

> I answer that it is about one's own 'thing', which *res* is unavoidably part and parcel of the Western Christian *res*, as inherited by a person whose perceptions are totally conditioned and limited by and dependent upon his being indigenous to this island. (*TA*, 11)

So Jones is here simultaneously claiming to be totally shaped by his being indigenous to the island of Britain (saying nothing about a British nationality, however), and claiming that his resultant cultural identity is nevertheless also inseparable from the Western Christian cultural identity. The *res* expressed by the poem is further conditioned, he continues, by the writer 'being a Londoner, of Welsh and English parentage, of Protestant upbringing, of Catholic subscription' (*TA*, 11). These autobiographical details are important for their role in shaping the content and form of the work, as he points out (*TA*, 11). Also important in this regard is his linguistic background, as he explains:

Though linguistically 'English m[...] owing to the accidents above mentioned [...] ases from the Welsh and Latin languages and a gre[...] Welsh and Romanic provenance have become part of the writer's *Realien*, w[...] a kind of Cockney setting. (*TA*, 11)

While admitting to a lack of grammatical expertise in the languages he is quoting from (*TA*, 11), he is concerned to justify the necessity of nevertheless using the original languages in these cases and not translating all terms into English. He explains over several pages (*TA*, 11–13) that the associations and images invoked by a particular word in a particular language are often not to be recaptured in the word's translation into another language: '"Tsar" will mean one thing and "Caesar" another to the end of time' (*TA*, 13). The use of untranslated words in languages such as Welsh and Latin, and to some extent French, German and Greek, alongside English, allows the poem to represent and embody the cultural reality which Jones proposes that it is meant to embody, that is the cultural complex of the island of Britain, which, as Jones argues, is a branch of the larger cultural complex of Western Europe.

From explaining the need to provide notes to elucidate various terms that he cannot be sure will be familiar to his readers, he is led to consider 'The Break' (*TA*, 15), a phenomenon he believes has happened in Western society, principally during the nineteenth century, and which has produced a difficulty in sign-making and sign-interpreting.[20] He mentions water as being an important part of the '*materia poetica*' (*TA*, 17) in Britain, due to local circumstances, and one which can be made to carry widely varying significations in a culture friendly to sign-making; he mentions as an aside that the modern understanding of such things as the molecular composition of water ought to be usable for purposes of poetic signifying, just as the

---

20 For a detailed discussion of 'The Break' in Jones' thinking, see Colin Wilcockson, 'David Jones and "The Break"', *Agenda* 15.2–3 (1977). See also A. C. Everatt, 'Doing and Making', in *David Jones: Diversity in Unity: Studies in his Literary and Visual Art*, Belinda Humphrey and Anne Price-Owen, eds (Cardiff: University of Wales Press, 2000), 70–1, who compares Jones' and Alasdair MacIntyre's understandings of 'The Break'.

English Metaphysical poets made scientific discoveries of their time part of their poetic matter. The implication though is that this is not happening to the extent that Jones would like to see it in his own time (*TA*, 16–18, 17 note 1). This discussion provides indications, however, of what Jones' own aim will be: to make locally, physically present elements represent larger meanings. Jones insists that, even though a poet of his time is no longer the official rememberer of its history for a tightly knit group as in previous ages, nevertheless even in what he sees as 'a late and complex phase of a phenomenally complex civilization' (*TA*, 21) the poet's task is still to recall 'something loved' (*TA*, 21) in the context of a given society – he gives the example of how a dog-rose can evoke associations in English people of summer in England, and 'moves something' in them 'at a deeper level than the Union Flag' (*TA*, 22). It is worth noting that here, as he generally does, he sees Englishness and Welshness as separate, as well as linked, and does not give weight to modern institutional British symbolism.

Jones explains the connection between the local and the universal further, pointing out that 'It is axiomatic that the function of the artist is to make things *sub specie aeternitatis*' (*TA*, 24), but that 'the works of man, unless they are of "now" and of "this place", can have no "for ever"' (*TA*, 24); in fact, taking things further, 'only what is actually loved and known can be seen *sub specie aeternitatis*' (*TA*, 24). This principle informs *The Anathemata*, as he has already indicated, but, to show that it is still possible to achieve this connection (between the local and the universal) in the art of his time, despite the obstacles he sees in terms of a lack of shared understanding of sign-making between the poet and the poet's audience, he cites James Joyce, who, an 'artist, while pre-eminently "contemporary" and indeed "of the future", was also of all artists the most of site and place' (*TA*, 26), and who, despite being 'most authentically the bard of the shapeless cosmopolis and of the megapolitan diaspora' (*TA*, 26), collected his historical material 'from the ancestral mound' (*TA*, 26). Thus in writing for his present through the particularities of the place and of the layers of the history of Dublin, Joyce has done for Ireland what Jones aims to do for Britain.[21]

---

21 Angela G. Dorenkamp, 'Time and Sacrament in *The Anathemata*', *Renascence* 23.4 (Summer 1971), 187, emphasizes Jones' concern to use signs that are valid for the time when he uses them.

After a long discussion of his art theory, Jones returns, towards the end of the preface, to give further indications as to his sources of inspiration: he suggests that he has often been set off on flights of imagination when attending Mass, and describes an example of such a train of thought, which he has had or may have had, on seeing a speck of dust or insect in a shaft of light. This beginning might, or possibly has, set him thinking, as he recounts, of Germanic halls, then the Vikings at York, then Canterbury, then Chaucer and the South Bank, then art galleries on the South Bank, then Battersea, the crossing of the Thames at Battersea during the Roman invasion and the ancient shield discovered in the river there, and then other works of ancient Celtic art also housed in the British museum (*TA*, 12). Jones' point here is to compare the short time it takes to follow such a chain of thought in the mind, and the much longer, more labour-laden time involved in following the same path geographically, or writing it. It is a revealing passage in terms of how his imagination makes associations, and again shows the inseparable connection of ancient history to the present day in his mind, and the combination of Germanic, Roman and Celtic ingredients in his vision of British culture, as well as hinting at the central placing of the liturgy among the themes of the poem.

Jones ends the preface with a long acknowledgement of sources, during which, as well as mentioning contemporaries who have helped him or whose books he has consulted, and various publications the authors of which he has forgotten or which are perhaps anonymous, he also acknowledges some of the 'more formidable and more forming creditors of the past' (*TA*, 39), again giving a sense of the shape of his cultural world. He mentions by name, among others, William Langland, Duns Scotus, St Thomas Aquinas, the writers of the French Arthurian romances, Gerald of Wales and St Anselm of Canterbury – a range of British figures of the various component nationalities, and figures from Latin countries but with connections to Britain. He also mentions general sources of influence, which he calls 'the basic things: the early mixed racial deposits, the myth (mythus) [there is a footnote here relating to why he uses the word "mythus", on the basis that "myth" may be understood as something necessarily fictional] that is specifically of this Island, and the Christian Liturgy, and Canon of the Scripture, and the Classical deposits' (*TA*, 40). This list repeats the oft-emphasized idea of the ethnic components of British culture (Celtic, Germanic and Latin, though not specified this time), its European background in the ancient Roman and Greek cultures, and the Christian religious background (with the Old Testament of the Bible introducing a Hebrew element, implied, but not specified, here). In the case of this list the 'basic things' seem to become more basic as the list progresses, so that the liturgy, introducing a metaphysical and divine framework, is the most fundamental, and those things closest to the surface are most specific and local to Britain.

A few childhood memories are also adduced as formative. These include books read by or to him, such as a children's version of the Arthur legends, Macaulay's *Lays of Ancient Rome*, and Keble's *Christian Year* with illustrations by Overbeck, all indicating the kind of interests (ancient and medieval legend, Christianity of a Catholic-leaning kind) which he retained, and which are incorporated into all his writings (*TA*, 41). He also recalls having the Welsh national anthem *Mae hen wlad fy nhadau* and another Welsh song *Ar hyd y nos* sung to him by his father (and failing to imitate the pronunciation) and being impressed by a reproduction of rare drawings of thirteenth-century Welsh soldiers (*TA*, 41): the themes of his fascination for Welsh things but difficulties with the language, and of his fascination with military matters, again having deep roots in his personal history, re-emerge here.

The poem itself contains seven named sections. The form of the poem is free, with no regular rhyme or metre, and with parts written as prose. The first section, 'Rite and Foretime', provides a liturgical, geological and prehistorical introduction and foundation for the rest of the poem.[22] It starts with the title, 'THE ANATHEMATA', subtitled by the quotation from the *Dies irae*, 'TESTE DAVID CUM SIBYLLA' (*TA*, 49, 68 note 3), a favourite quotation of Jones', which suggests Greek pagan and Hebrew elements making a common testimony to the Second Coming – Jones builds up a teleological view of history during the poem, according to which the events of the New Testament are the (earthly) culmination, but

---

22 Neil Corcoran, *The Song of Deeds: A Study of* The Anathemata *of David Jones* (Cardiff: University of Wales Press, 1982), 44–6, provides a useful summary of the themes of each of the sections of *The Anathemata*.

all pre-Christian stages of history help to make it possible, and derive their legitimacy from their place in the chain. Immediately following the title and subtitle the poem's first section starts with a description of a priest celebrating the Eucharistic liturgy, saying the words and making the gestures which occur just before the Consecration in the classical Roman rite, thus introducing the supernatural frame for the poem: the Mass also represents Jones' idea of an art work, as it is a sign, making the acts of the Crucifixion present again and revealing their timeless dimension, just as all art works, for Jones, bring the eternal out of the particular. The liturgical introduction leads on to topics of geological formation and prehistoric humanity which dominate the section. References of relevance to the British prehistorical dimension include the caves which in Welsh folklore contain sleeping heroes (*TA*, 55, 54 notes 5, 6) and the effects of the ice age in shaping the courses of rivers such as the Dee and the Severn (rivers that later connect Wales and England), and in moving, via glaciers, rocks from the area of the Clyde Estuary and Southern Uplands all the way down to Wales and the Midlands of England, a similar route to that taken by some Welsh legends, such as that of King Cole (*TA*, 69–70; 69 notes 1, 3; 70 note 4). These references knit together the parts of Britain now contained in England, Wales and Scotland, and the geological connection between southern Scotland and Wales parallels historical and literary connections emphasized elsewhere in Jones' work, such as the existence of the British kingdoms of the 'Old North' for some time after the Angle and Saxon invasions, the movement of Cunedda, the founder of the dynasty of the North Welsh princes, from what is now Scotland to what is now North Wales, and the ancient Welsh poem *Y Gododdin*, which is about a British battle group from an area in what is now Scotland, perhaps Edinburgh. The Cumbrian sheep count (numerals, often thought to be a Celtic survival, used by shepherds in the Lake District) is mentioned (*TA*, 77, 76 note 3), as is Arthur (*TA*, 79), carrying all the associations of Celtic British myth and legend we have discussed above. Jones also provides Mediterranean and European context for the British references: Troy (*TA*, 55–7; 54 notes 8, 9; 56 notes 1, 2, 3; 57 note 1) and Jerusalem are mentioned (*TA*, 58, 58 note 2), representing the legendary and religious foundations of Western culture. The Danube (*TA*, 59) and the Rhine (*TA*, 64) are included, the Danube named in German, the

Rhine presented at a stage when the Thames still flows into it, emphasizing the connection between Britain and the continent on a geographical level which Jones often foregrounds on a cultural level. So he has already in the prehistoric and foundational opening managed to include all those ethnic and cultural elements – Latin, Greek, Germanic, Celtic and Hebrew – which he sees as making up the Western European cultural complex, and the British cultural complex which is part of it.

The second section, 'Middle-Sea and Lear-Sea', portrays the Mediterranean foundations of British culture, and can be analysed as having two parts, the first naming elements in ancient Mediterranean civilization which contributed to the British cultural complex, and the second describing a sea voyage, departing from the ancient Eastern Mediterranean and arriving at the southern British shores, with the ship, among other things, representing the Church, and the captain Christ.[23] Of the ancient Mediterranean civilizations mentioned, Troy comes first (*TA*, 84), followed closely by the Roman Empire (*TA*, 85–90). A British connection is implied here, as both the Roman Empire and Britain are, according to legend, successor civilizations of Troy (*TA*, 54 note 8). Among aspects of Rome invoked are the 'Twelve Tables', originally ten, presented in such a way as to see them as a parallel to the biblical decalogue (*TA*, 85, 85 note 4), and the ceremony for the laying of the street grid in a new Roman town (*TA*, 87), perhaps intended to bring to mind the Roman foundation of London, as London plays an important role later in the poem. In the note to the reference to the 'Twelve Tables', Jones points out other parallels between Roman mythology and the Bible, and explains that Europeans have inherited both traditions, one through ethnic inheritance, and the other at a spiritual level, 'by "adoption and grace"' (*TA*, 85 note 4). This shows the levels of inheritance not only coexisting but also hierarchically arranged, with the Judaeo-Christian level overlaying the other inherited strata. Emphasis is also placed on the imperial aspect of Roman civilization ('"T's a great robbery/ – is empire' *TA*, 88, recalling St Augustine in *The City of God*, *TA*, 85 note 3), an emphasis which suggests again the British parallel, this time with the British

---

23   Corcoran, *The Song of Deeds*, 49, 52.

Empire of the time of his writing. Greeks, Egyptians and Hittites are also mentioned or alluded to (*TA*, 90–1), and the Greek references serve as a means to turn to the theme of the sea voyage, through the description of a number of famous Greek statues. The very early statue of a man carrying a calf is introduced, and its evocation of biblical images insisted on (*TA*, 91, 91 note 1), and then the 'Beautiful Kore', and its similarities to French Gothic carving are pointed out – Jones suggests too that the figure has a significance akin to that of other legendary beautiful women, such as the British Gwenhwyfar/Guinevere (*TA*, 92, 92 notes 1, 2). Jones makes the claim, in the body of the poem, that the sense of beauty displayed in these archaic Greek statues does not return until 'the Faustian lent' (*TA*, 92), meaning the Western Middle Ages. 'Faustian' is a term borrowed from Spengler to describe 'Celto-Latin-Germanic-Western-Christian culture' (*TA*, 92, note 4). Mention is also made of the Thomistic theory of beauty, '*splendor formarum*' (*TA*, 93, 93 note 1), giving an indication as to Jones' philosophical allegiance. There is then a jump in time from the archaic 'to the skill-years' (*TA*, 93), and he describes what seem to be Phidias' two giant statues of Athena in Athens, but with no explanatory footnote this time; he makes the description, however, using a number of phrases which in Catholic contexts refer to the Virgin Mary (for example, 'tower of ivory', 'house of gold', *TA*, 94). The link of associations from Athena to the Virgin Mary to the Star of the Sea (a title of the Virgin Mary) allows the introduction of the ship, its crew-members a mix of Greeks and Phoenicians, again suggesting the dual classical and biblical foundations of Western culture (*TA*, 105 note 2), a ship which makes the voyage from the Aegean to the southern shores of Britain, rounding Iberia and Brittany. A strong emphasis is laid on a number of geographical features which may be intended to be corresponding pairs, one element in the Mediterranean and one in Britain: so, for example, the Aegean with its islands may be intended as a parallel to the Scilly Isles, and the Cape of Sounion may be echoed by Cornwall. Greek and Celtic mythology also correspond: for example, the sea gods Poseidon and Manannan. The prominent showing of Cornwall also facilitates the introduction of the Celtic dimension to the linguistic, historical and cultural allusions.

Towards the end of the section, Jones again places his Latin, Greek, Semitic, Celtic and Germanic cultural web in the light of an overarching religious idea: in this case, he recalls the priest's offering of the Mass on behalf, as Jones explains in a note, of all humanity, and even all sentient creation, and perhaps insentient too (*TA*, 106, 106 note 2). Jones' vision here is important in relation to the question of nationality, in that he sees the human participants of all cultural phases as having, at least potentially, been redeemed by the events of the New Testament – thus every stage of human development has its eternal significance, as well as being part of a story leading to present cultural configurations. Interestingly, Waugh, in *Helena*, presents the Western view of the Redemption as being one directed solely at rational beings, therefore not at the rest of nature. Jones here adopts the view that nature as a whole might be redeemed, which Waugh attributes to Eastern Christianity. Jones ascribes a bureaucratic mentality to the Roman Empire, but does not bring out any notion of the benign rationalism of Western civilization, as Waugh does, or any idea of pragmatism as a permanent feature of British culture, as again, Waugh seems to (though an element of deliberate anachronism may account for Waugh's attribution of pragmatism to Ancient Britons in the case of *Helena*). For Jones, the British pragmatism seen in *In Parenthesis* is part of the utilitarian attitude associated with empire.

'Angle-Land', the short third section, imagines the ship moving further along the southern coast of Britain, and eventually towards London. It presents the arrival of the Germanic Angles, Saxons and Jutes in Britain, and their gradual displacing of Celtic Britons in what became England.[24] The time when there was still a coexistence of Britons and Anglo-Saxons in the same area is remembered by allusion, for example, to the experience of the Angle hermit St Guthlac, who took surviving Brythonic-speakers in the fens for devils (*TA*, 112, 112 note 3), and Jones also notes the loss of the Roman-based civilization among the Britons, who have found themselves driven into remote areas ('*cives* gone wold-men', *TA*, 113). The section ends with a renewed evocation of the geographical connection of Britain

24 Corcoran, *The Song of Deeds*, 55.

with the European continent, describing how all the east-flowing rivers of Britain mingle with the Rhine in the North Sea. 'Angle-Land' as a whole suggests that, in the formation of England, there is likely to have been some mixing of Britons and Anglo-Saxons, rather than simply displacement of the former by the latter.

'Redriff', the fourth section, is even shorter. In it the poet imagines that the ship from the Mediterranean turns into the Thames estuary and docks, and it features Eb Bradshaw, maternal grandfather of Jones, who worked in Thames-side shipbuilding – he is requested to repair the ship in an economizing, utilitarian manner, but refuses, as Jones here defends the right and duty of the artist when engaged in any 'making' to produce the best possible work.[25] In celebrating the port activity of the Thames, Jones is drawing attention to a formative element in London's history and that of Britain as a whole, and he is showing how the accumulation of influences and people through maritime travel and transport has contributed to the making of the island culture. He is also practising his principle that the poet should use the material that he or she knows: Jones grew up in south-east London, and was very familiar with the Thames shore east of the City.

The long fifth section 'The Lady of the Pool' could be regarded as the heart of the poem, and concentrates on the figure of Elen Monica, the London lavender seller, who represents all womanhood. She talks to the Mediterranean ship's captain, discoursing on various locations in London and on the other men she has met on their way through.[26] Here Jones has created the opportunity to present the mythical and legendary background of London in considerable detail.[27] The central role of London in the poem reflects both Jones' own London origins and London's central place in the development of the national culture: as a principal port and urban centre of the island during the greater part, if not all, of recorded history, a large proportion of the peoples and influences entering the island have passed

---

25   Corcoran, *The Song of Deeds*, 56–7.
26   Blamires, in *David Jones: Artist and Writer*, 143, notes how different historical periods mix 'almost imperceptibly' in this section.
27   Corcoran, *The Song of Deeds*, 58–9.

through it. This is marked in Jones' own genealogy by an Italian element in his mother's background. The section is saturated with allusions related to the various components of London's myth and legend. A representative sample will serve to bring out the pattern Jones creates. The idea that 'What's under works up' (*TA*, 164) runs through many of the allusions. London's alluvial soil (*TA*, 163–4) is linked to traditions of buried sleeping Celtic guardian figures: Brân, whose head, according to the Welsh legend, is buried under the White Hill, that is the Tower of London, and protects the whole island, as well as various other figures, including Arthur (*TA*, 163–4, 163 note 3, 164 note 2). Elen Monica associates this protection of the guardians with the fact that 'THIS BOROUGH WERE NEVER FORCED' (*TA*, 163), a statement which Dilworth sees as a reference to the Second World War bombardment of London, which Jones witnessed.[28] The influence of the legendary Celtic guardian figures rises from underneath to make its mark on such much later English writers as Shakespeare and Milton, Jones notes (*TA*, 163 note 3). The subterranean theme extends to the mention of a number of medieval London churches and archaeological finds beneath them which reveal pre-Christian religious uses of the sites: for example, St Paul's was traditionally believed to be on the site of a temple to Jupiter or Diana (*TA*, 127, 126 note 12), St Peter-upon-Cornhill (*TA*, 160–1, 160–1 note 3) may have been on or near a pagan site (and has legendary associations with King Cole), a sculpture of the *Deae Matres* (mother goddesses) was found on the site of the Church of the Crutched Friars, Aldgate (*TA*, 162, 162 note 3). Other references to the Welsh substrate in London legend include King Lud, popularly associated with Ludgate, featuring as Lludd in the Welsh story of Lludd and Llefelys (*TA*, 124, 124 note 1, 167 note 2). The medieval statues of the giants Gog and Magog, protectors of the City of London, are commemorated and Jones explains their earlier designation as Goemagot and Corenius, figures from a Roman-British myth involving the Emperor Diocletian's daughters and a Trojan hero – a story which may have been influenced by the legend of Britain's foundation by a descendant of the Trojan Aeneas (*TA*, 167–8, 168 note 1).

---

28 Thomas Dilworth, *Reading David Jones* (Cardiff: University of Wales Press, 2008), 155.

The fact that in Roman times London was the capital of the Trinobantes, the British tribe occupying the areas where Essex and Middlesex now are, and that it continued to be regarded as associated with Essex under the Saxons, is alluded to and explained (*TA*, 133, 133 note 3). Helen, mother of the Emperor Constantine and wife of Constantius Chlorus, is included (*TA*, 131, 131 note 3), bringing with her Roman and Celtic British associations, and Constantius Chlorus is referred to in his own right, as reliever of London, who is commemorated on a Roman medallion (*TA*, 134, 134 note 1). The reactions of an English sailor and a Welsh sailor to an annoyance are compared. The English sailor uses bad language while the Welsh one uses oaths involving a series of Welsh historical and legendary motifs (*TA*, 149–52) – this scene resembles a similar comparison of Welsh and English reactions in *In Parenthesis*. The connection between the Welsh dragon and the dragon as a Roman military symbol, a favourite theme of Jones, is introduced again (*TA*, 154, 154 note 3). Jones, through Roger Bacon, alludes to the idea that the English have always been nominalist or empiricist in philosophy (*TA*, 158–9, 159 note 1) – an observation which connects with the way that Jones presents the English sailor as more pragmatic than the Welsh sailor with his long cultural memory, and also the similar way in which he contrasts Welsh and English soldiers in *In Parenthesis*. A Viking component is included through, for example, reference to the Saga of Olaf the Saint, which describes medieval London (*TA*, 146, 146 note 2, 161 note 3). The Scottish late medieval poet Dunbar's poem *In Honour of the City of London* is included (*TA*, 162, 162 note 6), ensuring that all three nations of the Island of Britain are woven into the texture. Towards the end of the section, a priest is described saying the Latin liturgy with a cockney accent (*TA*, 165), thus combining the local with the universal, in accordance with Jones' theory of art. So, this section uses London as the specific locality through which to build up once again the British myth, highlighting the contributions of the same ethnic groups (Semitic, Greek, Roman, Celtic, Germanic) as he does elsewhere, emphasizing the Mediterranean origins of British culture, using geological metaphors, moving back and forth through history, and casting the whole structure in the light of a religious narrative.

The sixth section, 'Keel, Ram, Stauros', portrays the return journey of the Mediterranean ship to Greece, from London to Athens, as well as exploring the cultural and religious symbolism of the tree trunk.[29] Themes from earlier sections, such as London mythology (for example, various possibilities for the etymology of Billingsgate, *TA*, 170, 170 note 1), and sea mythology (for example, ancient names for parts of the North Sea, *TA*, 170–1, 171 note 1), mixing Celtic, Germanic and Mediterranean elements, recur in reduced form in what is a relatively short section. The introduction of the motif of the cross prepares for the religious emphasis of the final two sections.

'Mabinog's Liturgy', the long seventh section, is based on the shape of the Roman Eucharistic liturgy (the Mass), highlighting the parallels between a celebration of the liturgical ritual and the events of the New Testament, with a particular emphasis on the Nativity, and, as always, weaving in historical and mythological allusions from the cultural history of Western Europe and its Mediterranean foundations. The idea of the beginning of the sixth and last age of the world (the sixth of the seven ages of the world in medieval historical thinking), dating from the birth of John the Baptist, is prominent in this section (*TA*, 211, 211 note 1, 219, 218 note 5). Once more the theme of nationality is a key concern. Among the most relevant allusions to this are the initial reference to evidence that Celts from Asia Minor were part of the Roman Army in Egypt, together with comment on the origins of Celtic culture by the Rhine, in what is now south-west Germany, and on the fact that the Celts were succeeded by the Teutons as the bogeymen of the Roman Empire (*TA*, 185, 184 notes 1, 4, 5). Jones at the same time notes that some groups among the British Celts were partially Romanized even before the invasion (*TA*, 185, 184 note 7). With this set of allusions, Jones sets up, via Celtic culture, the connection between Britain, Germanic Europe, the Roman Empire and the eastern Mediterranean. He also reiterates his oft-asserted point that British culture is a product and branch of wider European culture. The links from the Middle East to Britain are of special relevance in this section because of its concentration on the liturgy and the New Testament. Further references

---

29   Corcoran, *The Song of Deeds*, 65.

to the Roman-ness of Britain come through the Second Legion, which was stationed in Britain for several hundred years (*TA*, 219, 218 note 3) – the motif of Roman legionaries from Britain is expanded in the poems of *The Sleeping Lord*[30] to embrace Roman legionaries in Britain stationed in Palestine. The words 'Mair' (Welsh for 'Mary') and 'ymherawdr' (Welsh for 'emperor') are included as unbroken links between Latin words used in Britain during Roman times and contemporary speech in Britain, via intermediate Old Welsh forms, and, in the case of Mair, a link is made to the first arrival of Christianity in Britain through the Roman Empire (*TA*, 217, 217 note 5, 219, 218 note 6). The continued use of the Roman Calends in Welsh ('Calan Mai' being the first of May and 'Calan Gaeaf' the first of November) provides another such link of continuity between contemporary culture in Britain and the culture of the Roman Empire (*TA*, 190, 190 note 3, 195, 195 note 4). He highlights the officialdom and bureaucracy of the Roman Empire (*TA*, 186–7), another motif which is expanded on in the poems of *The Sleeping Lord*, in which Roman bureaucracy recalls British Imperial bureaucracy.[31] The continuity of imperial etiquette with ceremonial forms of the Church (such as candles and chasubles) is a related point which Jones makes during this section (*TA*, 199, 199 note 2, 202, 202 note 2). Among other references relevant to nationality are, once again, Arthur (*TA*, 197–8, 197 note 1, 198 note 1), Oxford as centre of the island and centre of learning (*TA*, 211, 211 notes 3, 4, 5), three witches representing England, Wales and Scotland (*TA*, 215), and the concept of anamnesis (with a sacramental meaning, and, for Jones, describing the function of art), which does not just cause remembrance of something absent, but makes something present (*TA*, 205, 205 note 1). So this is a section emphasizing continuities, from the Roman Empire to modern Britain, from the Roman Empire to the Church, between Britain and the Middle East via the Celts, via the Roman Empire, and via the Church – also, on a more metaphysical level, between history and liturgy.

30   David Jones, *The Sleeping Lord and Other Fragments* (London: Faber, 1995) (*SL*). Further references to this edition are given after quotations in the text.
31   Staudt, *At the Turn of a Civilization*, 120, sees Spengler's view that first-century Roman civilization is parallel to mid-twentieth-century Western civilization as 'implicit' in *The Anathemata*.

The final section, 'Sherthursdaye and Venus Day', continues the movement through the liturgy of the Mass started in 'Mabinog's Liturgy', but with the focus in terms of New Testament history on the Passion, rather than on the Nativity (hence the name, referring to Maundy Thursday and the Last Supper, and Good Friday and the Crucifixion).[32] Among the many allusions, the geography of the Holy Land is important, and Welsh geography is sometimes paralleled with it: the hills of north-west Wales, which Jones' father could see from where he grew up, are compared to the hills of Jerusalem (*TA*, 233, 233 note 1), and various Welsh bodies of water are linked to the Pool of Bethesda and other biblical occurrences of the water motif (*TA*, 235–8, 234 notes 5, 6, 7). As well as Jones' belief that culture develops from specific localities and their geography, these passages show water as a carrier of multiple significations, including its role in the sacraments, as the necessary material element in baptism, and as a constituent of the bread and wine needed for the Eucharist, as he explains (*TA*, 236 note 1). Hills have a significance as burial mounds ('Sion tumulus', *TA*, 241), and in this connection the Arthurian legends are invoked, recalling the motif of sleeping buried heroes from Celtic legend, which parallels the Resurrection (*TA*, 225–6, 225 note 1, 226 note 1, 242). The three peoples of the West, Latin, Celtic and Germanic, are mentioned again, '*et gentium, cenhedloedd und Völker*', and in a footnote Jones explains that as a person from the West one can only 'apprehend' in the modes associated with these ethnic identities, although other strands, Greek and Judaean, contribute to their cultural foundations (*TA*, 241, 241 note 2). Jones also includes his Spenglerian view that the West is in decline: 'Failing/ (finished ?) West/ your food, once' (*TA*, 231). This quotation comes after what seems to be a reference to the wars of the twentieth century, and between allusions to agriculture and the Eucharist – so the decline of the West may be attributed here to the decline of attachment to the sacrament. These references show that the poem covers history up to Jones' own time. The connection of the idea of 'sacrament' with the Roman military oath of loyalty is noted too (*TA*, 228, 228 note 4), making the same point as in the previous section that there is a continuity of forms between the Roman Empire and the

32   Corcoran, *The Song of Deeds*, 70.

Church – the idea of the British Empire and the Church as inheritors of the Roman Empire, but in different ways, is a key theme of poems in *The Sleeping Lord*. There are also tributes to Gerard Manley Hopkins, the poet who, as we have seen, Jones considers to be particularly representative of the British (English and Welsh) artistic spirit: there is an acknowledged quotation from the poem 'As kingfishers catch fire' in the passage on water, 'roundy wells' (*TA*, 235, 234 note 12), and there also appears to be oblique reference to the same poem in a long passage in which Jones affirms that various birds, especially crows, act according to their divinely given specific nature. Hopkins' poem is on kingfishers and other beings expressing their selves in this way.[33]

The Anathemata, the most complex of Jones' works, recapitulates the themes of *In Parenthesis*, but adds a more explicit cosmic framework. In terms of the nationality issue, the constant motif of the Celtic, Latin and Germanic background of British civilization, as well as of Western European civilization, emerges clearly, as do Britain's links with the eastern Mediterranean, and with the Classical and biblical worlds. A striking aspect of *The Anathemata* is that an epic of British nationality and history, starting from the history's beginnings, and reaching, in a gently hinted at rather than very explicit way, to the present, is poetically conceived within an overarching Catholic metaphysical framework. Jones conceives of his sacramental world-view as capable of making sense of all levels and stages of British history, whether pre-Christian or post-Reformation.

The Sleeping Lord and Other Fragments

The Sleeping Lord and Other Fragments is a collection of shorter poems, although only one ('A, a, a, Domine Deus') is short enough to fit on a single page. Of the nine poems in the collection eight are substantially related to

---

33 Gerard Manley Hopkins, *The Major Works*, Catherine Phillips, ed. (Oxford: Oxford University Press, 1986), 129.

the nationality theme. The collection first appeared in 1974, but contains poems published earlier. Many of them were written during the 1960s, but earlier material is also included. Most portray either Roman soldiers or scenes from Welsh legend. Jones generally reworks the same complex material in all his writings, but a significant development, which is relevant to three of the poems ('The Dream of Private Clitus', 'The Fatigue' and 'The Tribune's Visitation'), is the idea of Roman soldiers, who in some cases may be from Britain, being stationed in Jerusalem, and even witnessing the events of the New Testament, an idea which derived from his seeing British soldiers in Jerusalem on his 1934 visit there, during the British Mandate period – a visit he describes, together with its influence on him, in a letter to Welsh writer Saunders Lewis (*Dai G*, 56–7). The association of British imperial soldiers with those of the Roman Empire is of course already present in *The Anathemata*, as Jones himself points out in his letter to Saunders Lewis. The first poem of the collection, 'A, a, a, Domine Deus', is the only one not to touch on nationality, addressing Jones' difficulty in finding significance, as an artist, in the products of modern industrial civilization.

'The Wall' is written as if from the point of view of sentries on the walls of Rome, for most of the poem: it is actually a fragment taken from a longer writing, which shows the sentries at the walls of Roman Jerusalem, as Jones explains in the preface to 'The Fatigue' (*SL*, 24). The theme of Roman soldiers in Jerusalem is to be found in the following three poems, and in Jones' symbolism different cities can stand for each other, especially Rome, Jerusalem and London. The mention of the hills of Rome (*SL*, 12) in particular recalls the hills of Jerusalem and London which appear elsewhere in Jones' work (for example in *The Anathemata*). The phrase 'the walls that maintain the world' (*SL*, 10), while referring to the walls of the city of Rome, suggests a similar idea to that of the walls round the Roman Empire, which are a key part of the symbolism of Waugh's novel *Helena*. The 'pontifex' (*SL*, 10), the high priest in pagan Rome, is referred to early, but the word also recalls one of the titles of the Pope, 'Pontifex Maximus'. The legendary connection between Rome and Troy is referred to as well (*SL*, 11), a connection which, in the context of Jones' poetry, reminds the reader that Britain also has a Trojan origin by legend. Britain is brought into the poem explicitly when the narrating soldier remembers a captured

British leader he has seen in Rome, using British Celtic and Anglo-Saxon vocabulary for 'king' and 'land' ('the dying *tegernos* of the wasted *landa*', *SL*, 11), representing the Celtic and Germanic ethnicities, and mentioning his 'dappled patria' – Hopkins' poem 'Pied Beauty' and Jones' theory on the dappledness of British art ('An Aspect of the Art of England', *The DG*, 59–62) are thereby recalled. The soldiers describe their utensils in such a way as to echo the routine, portrayed in *In Parenthesis*, of British soldiers in the First World War ('… the sooted billikin/ brews the night broth', *SL*, 13). The rituals of Roman town planning are described again (*SL*, 12–13), important to Jones not only as a ritual, and therefore a sign-making activity, but also because the uniform plan of the Roman city or even camp underlies many towns and cities in all lands which the Romans occupied, including Palestine and Britain, as well as Italy. A theme which recurs through much of the poem is that of the military Roman empire having become commercial ('the shopkeepers presume to make/ the lupine cry their own', *SL*, 11), and the connected associations between the City, Empire, and robbery ('robber walls of the world city', *SL*, 14), recalling Saint Augustine's *City of God*. The City and Empire being set up for war ('did they parcel out … the *civitas* of God/ that we should sprawl/ from Septimontium/ a megalopolis that wills death?', *SL*, 13) forms a parallel with the City of London and the British Empire, the word 'shopkeepers' connecting with Napoleon's famous remark, and the word 'megalopolis' indicating modern civilization. Thus the Roman Empire has two heirs: the Church, which inherits some of its forms and titles, but is an empire on a spiritual level, and the British Empire, or indeed any subsequent worldly empire which mixes war and commerce (the contrast being the one which Saint Augustine made between the earthly city and the heavenly city). Late in the poem the two sides of earthly empire are emphasized, that of war and that of peace and commercial prosperity, combined in 'armed peace' (*SL*, 14), and, emblematic of this paradox, Mars' ancestry as an agricultural god is alluded to. The soldiers talk of the 'Gauls and gods' (*SL*, 14) they have helped to die. The dying Gaul for Jones represents the survival of artistic and religious culture in the face of bureaucratic and utilitarian suppression, and is also emblematic of Christ's Crucifixion (and, by implication, Resurrection). Given Jones' Spenglerian conviction that the British Empire of his time had reached the same stage of development as the late Roman Empire, a bureaucratic phase soon to be followed by collapse, this mention of dying Gauls and gods towards the end of the poem seems to hint at a collapse of the British Empire but perhaps also at a future transfiguration of some of its forms, just as Roman forms survived in the Church when the Empire collapsed.

'The Dream of Private Clitus' is, as Jones explains in its preface, a fragment of what was intended to be a longer work (*SL*, 15), and mainly takes the form of short prose paragraphs. It is the recounting of a dream by a Roman soldier, Clitus, from the region of Rome, to his comrade, Oenomaus, from Greece, while both are guarding the walls of Jerusalem at the time of the Passion (*SL*, 15), although what appears of the poem itself does not make it clear that that is where they are. The dream was dreamt by Clitus during a German campaign, while he was sharing a bivouac with a former comrade, a Celt, Lugobelinos, a name which later developed into Llewelyn in Welsh, and who was subsequently killed during the fighting against the Germans (*SL*, 15). Most obviously, Jones is again pointing out the ethnic diversity of the Roman Empire, as he acknowledges in the preface (*SL*, 15), and in this way reminding the reader of the influences which have gone towards forming the West, and, in various ways, Britain. There are strong echoes of the First World War again in this poem, with twentieth-century British military slang, and the motif of the Celtic soldier fighting against German opponents. The setting of the site where the dream occurred at the 'Limes Germanicus' (*SL*, 16), which appears in the first line, will recall to the reader of Waugh's *Helena* the section of the novel set along the defensive line in just this area, and the conversation between Helena and Constantius about the significance of the walls of the Empire – Clitus later speaks of himself as having been encamped 'beyond the walls of the world' (*SL*, 18). Clitus' thinking that the interspersed branches of the forest look like pointed arches, even though, as he admits, he has never seen such a thing in stone (*SL*, 16–17), is an allusion to later cultural developments in Northern Europe, and Lugobelinos' calling an eagle he sees 'the Roman bird' (*SL*, 17) may be meant to bring to mind the symbol of the Holy Roman Empire as well. Lugobelinos is a thoroughly Romanized Celt ('Now, Celt or no, my Lugo fancied his weight as an inmate of our Asylum and reckoned himself as Ilian and as Urban as the Twins' *SL*, 16), which reminds the reader not only of the strong Roman influence on Britain, but also of the way that the British Empire included anglicized members from outside Britain. What Clitus sees in his dream is a vision of the carving of the Tellus Mater goddess on the Ara Pacis Augustae monument in Rome, in which the carving reaches out and touches him (*SL*, 15, 19–20). The Tellus Mater seems to represent agriculture and, thereby, civilization, the prerequisites for the Christian sacraments, as Jones often points out. Lugobelinos in the dream cries out the Welsh mythical name 'Modron', which, as Clitus understands, is the equivalent of 'Matrona', and also 'Porth-Annwfn', meaning, as Clitus also understands, the 'porta', or gate, of the underworld (*SL*, 20) – the strong connection between Latin and Welsh language and mythology is brought out here. Clitus' vision is interrupted when he is awakened by Brasso, a 'fact-man' (*SL*, 21), who represents the bureaucratic, utilitarian and, as Jones sees it, anti-artistic forces characteristic of late civilizations, whether Roman or Western. The poem concludes with Clitus speculating on the situation that will pertain when 'the Urbs falls' (*SL*, 23). This brings to mind the future fall of the Roman Empire, and also that of the British Empire and Western civilization, which Jones believed he was witnessing.

'The Fatigue' is another fragment dealing with Roman troops of international origins guarding the walls of Roman Jerusalem. This time the troops' presence in Jerusalem is made explicit in the fragment, as is the time, which coincides with the Passion. As Jones specifies in the preface to 'The Fatigue', he is imagining some of the soldiers to be Gaulish or British Celts (*SL*, 23). The poem portrays a party of soldiers being selected and sent to take part in the Crucifixion. As always in Jones' poems with Roman military themes, there is a mixture of Roman and First World War military terminology, establishing the parallel between the periods. In the course of the poem, among references which strengthen the links Jones wants to show, the Catullevani are mentioned, the British semi-Romanized people (of whom Cunobelinos, Shakespeare's Cymbeline, was king), who were thriving at the time of the Passion and who faced the early Roman landings in Britain, which took place slightly later (*SL*, 31, 31 note 1). Jones here, again, shows the British as the colonized, rather than the colonizers as they were to be in his time. He introduces a multi-ethnic network of cultural allusions to refer to the Crucifixion itself, including the Anglo-Saxon poem 'The Dream of the Rood', the Roman liturgy, the Aeneid, and even the Havamal from Old Norse mythology (*SL*, 32, notes 1, 3, 6, 7). Britain is referred to again by the suggestion of the use of a 'bascauda' (British-made basket) to carry nails in (*SL*, 33, 33 note 3), and by the mention of a Briton present, 'Ginger the Mountain', who was originally captured as a slave (*SL*, 37, 37 note 2). The connection between ancient Roman insignia and later ecclesiastical costumes and practices is made again by means of the mention of 'infullae', a kind of ceremonial head-band which has been retained as the ribbons hanging from the back of the bishop's mitre (*SL*, 35 note 1). The latter part of the poem (*SL*, 38–41) concentrates on the central bureaucracy in Rome and the way that orders emerge from the imperial bureaucratic machinery in a impersonal way: in case the reader does not make the connection with the British imperial military bureaucracy of his own time Jones hints in a footnote, 'In writing this part of "The Fatigue" the similarity between "then" and "now" was not far from my mind' (*SL*, 38 note 3).

'The Tribune's Visitation' is, as its short preface explains, again about the Roman army in Palestine, but is not specific about the exact time: some time 'in the earlier decades of the First Century AD' (*SL*, 45); while the soldiers belong to 'the Italica cohort' but are again 'of mixed recruitment' (*SL*, 45). The piece is a speech of encouragement by a visiting tribune to the soldiers (and includes some responses). It again makes the situation stand, in addition, for British military scenes of the twentieth century by devices,[34] such as having privates give their number and name (*SL*, 47), and by blending the idea of someone being from inner Rome with his being cockney: 'and you good Cockney bred/ born well in sound of the geese-cry' (*SL*, 46); this same 'cockney' soldier has also fought previously 'On the German *limes*' (*SL*, 46). References to Britain from the Roman point of view, however, call it 'unstable Britain' and talk of 'druid bangors farside the Gaulish Strait' (*SL*, 48), giving a sense of the change of roles Britain has undergone, having been an unruly and outer province of an

---

34 See also Christine Pagnoulle, *David Jones: A Commentary on some Poetic Fragments* (Cardiff: University of Wales Press, 1987), 59.

empire in ancient times. However, the mention of the 'druid bangors' also points to the continuity of the Celtic bardic tradition, in some form, into modern Welsh poetry. When mentioning the 'druid bangors', the tribune is promising to speak as a 'forthright Roman', although he claims that he could 'out-poet ovates from druid bangors farside the Gaulish Strait', having been taught how by 'my Transpadane grandma's friend' (*SL*, 48) – a friend likely to be a Celt as well if from Transpadane Gaul. So here the ancient Roman and modern English self-estimation as pragmatic and to-the-point are contrasted with what they see as the poetic and mystical, perhaps unreliable, tendencies of the peoples of less central, and, more specifically, Celtic, regions.[35] The tribune's speech turns into a diatribe against localism, in favour of the empire:

>   It's the world-bounds
>   we're detailed to beat
>   to discipline the world-floor
>   to a common level
>   till everything presuming difference
>   and all the sweet remembered demarcations
>   wither
>   to the touch of us
>   and know the fact of empire (*SL*, 50–1)

The tribune is shown representing a utilitarian attitude ('We are men of now and must strip as the facts of now would have it', *SL*, 51–2), and he regards local rituals as out of date – 'for the young-time' (*SL*, 50). The phrase 'young-time' recalls Jones' semi-Spenglerian vision of the growth and decay of eras of civilization, so the parallel is here again clear between the utilitarian Roman Empire and the modern utilitarian civilization of Jones' time. According to the tribune, any local loyalty, even to Italy, must be suppressed, as it could lead to empathy with people whose places they may be ordered to conquer, such as the British Celts, whose 'Ordovician hills' (*SL*, 55), hills now in central Wales (*SL*, 55 note 2), have not yet been

---

35 Pagnoulle, *David Jones: A Commentary*, 41–2, notes that in these poems the Celts are regarded by the Romans with suspicion, as otherworldly rather than utilitarian.

but are soon to be included in the Empire. The tribune's speech ends with an evocation of the family they all belong to, loyalty to which he recommends, namely Caesar's army, and this passage is full of striking uses of language with ecclesiastical significance: for example, the '*sacramentum*' (*SL*, 56), the oath which Roman soldiers took on joining the army, is mentioned as binding the members of the army together, an idea which recalls the way that the Church's sacraments bind the members of the Church together. Eucharistic echoes are also present, in the form of bread being broken and a cup shared, and the idea of rebirth is included, in this case rebirth from Caesar (*SL*, 58). So the Roman Empire in this poem has a double signification: in its earthly form it recurs as another imperial civilization, the modern West, with its utilitarian lack of sensibilities, and its aiming at efficiency in pursuit of immediate goals. The Roman Empire is also, however, succeeded, at a spiritual level, by the Church, which offers a universal spiritual allegiance, but which, unlike Empire, can, and as Jones would see it, must, coexist with local earthly pieties.

The following poem, 'The Tutelar of the Place', which Jones describes as a 'companion piece' to 'The Tribune's Visitation' (*SL*, 45), is a prayer to a female supernatural figure to protect the sense of the local against the levelling tendencies of utilitarian civilization: it does not directly address British-related issues, although it does include a smattering of Welsh vocabulary. However, as noted elsewhere, Jones believes that art must start from the local and move from there to the universal, and this is his method in his own work, thus the idea of protecting local particularity against levelling is a crucial element in his oeuvre, and the significance of the cultures of the island of Britain for him are as ways to reach transcendental significance (as any other local cultures may be for those who know them), rather than ends in themselves.

'The Hunt', as Jones observes in a final note (*SL*, 69), is based on the hunt for the Boar Trwyth by war-bands led by Arthur in the medieval Welsh tale 'Culhwch ac Olwen'. This is a favourite motif for the poet, and he makes it relevant to the general theme of nationality by emphasizing the idea of dappledness in his description of Arthur, 'the speckled lord of Prydain [Britain]' (*SL*, 68), in an injured and dishevelled state after having ridden through the forest – a dappled quality is usually associated by Jones with British art, as he argues in the essay 'An Aspect of the Art of England' (*The DG*, 59–62). Perhaps in support of his view that British culture is not conceivable in isolation from neighbouring continental cultures he draws attention to the presence of continental contingents in the hunt taking place in South Wales (*SL*, 65, 65 note 3).

'The Sleeping Lord', one of the longer poems in the collection, is based on the recurrent theme, in Jones' work, of buried heroes in the island of Britain, and the landscape of Wales, especially South Wales, figures prominently; much Welsh vocabulary is used for geographical features. In this case the starting point is the body of a palaeolithic young person, found in a cave on the Gower Peninsula: Jones points out in the footnote that the period of this burial is from long before Britain became an island, and he thus draws attention, as he frequently does, to Britain's continental links (*SL*, 71, 71 note 2). The early section of the poem has a strong geological element, like the first part of *The Anathemata*. Jones sees the body as that of a young prince, and by reference to the idea of his having a foot-bearer, and then a candle-bearer, he makes a transition to the court of a British or Welsh leader from the sub-Roman or medieval period. The leader's hall is imagined, with the Laws of Hywel Dda as a source of information about how such a hall would be organized (*SL*, 78 note 2). The blessing of the priest before the meal is represented and this introduces a new theme: the priest silently remembers, with the purpose of praying for them, all those who have died, including the clergy of Britain, its rulers and warriors, the general people of Britain, and people of the world 'from the unknown beginnings/ unguessed millenniums back/ until now' (*SL*, 86). As always, Jones is here placing the particular in a universal context. The priest's recollection includes a number of digressions. One involves the scene of an abandoned port, littered with the remnants of trade – this appears to be a reference to the collapse of the Roman Empire in Britain, and is also likely to be meant to bring to mind twentieth-century destruction in Western civilization. Similar imagery is used in the poem 'Prothalamion' in *Wedding Poems*,[36] to describe the effects of bombing in London during the Second

---

36   David Jones, *Wedding Poems*, Thomas Dilworth, ed. (London: Enitharmion, 2002) (*WP*). Further references to this edition are given after quotations in the text.

World War. Under the heading of leaders the priest recalls a number of historical and legendary figures of the sub-Roman period who occur frequently in Jones' oeuvre, such as Cunedda Wledig, Emrys Wledig and 'Elen the daughter of Coil' (*SL*, 85). Jones suggests the early connections between Britain and Christianity by having the priest mention an early Christian writer who originated in Britain, 'Faustus called "of Regensium"' (*SL*, 82), and other Christian and Celtic links are mentioned during a digression on Irenaeus, who came from close to Galatia (in Asia Minor), 'where there are men that speak the same tongue as the men of the Island' (*SL*, 83), and who knew Polycarp, who knew the Apostle John, 'that the men of the Island call Ieuan or Ioan' (*SL*, 84). Jones also indicates the way he sees the priest and the poet as practising related disciplines: he has the priest compare his own activity in recalling with that of the household bards, and shows him approving of their love for the 'things of the Island', even if he doubts their factual accuracy: 'he was dubious about much that these poets asserted though they were indeed most skilled artists and remembrancers & conservators of the things of the Island' (*SL*, 82). The priest imagines too the four Gospels as a sacred version of the four branches of the Mabinogi. Jones thus presents the New Testament as the fulfilment of Celtic legend (*SL*, 84, 84 notes 3, 4, 5, 6).

The following section portrays the hunt for the Boar Trwyth, a favourite motif, but here the emphasis is on the idea of destruction. There are quotations from the ancient Welsh poem mourning the destruction of the hall of Cynddylan in Shrewsbury by the Angles (*SL*, 88, 88 note 4), and from Ennius lamenting the destruction of forest (*SL*, 89, 89 note 1). The description of the destruction wrought by the Boar Trwyth is followed by an evocation of the pollution of the rivers of south-east Wales: a shift in time has occurred, as the results of modern industrialization are lamented here. The poem then moves back in time to imagine the medieval English garrison of the English-Welsh border castle at Hay-on-Wye being disturbed by a sound caused by a movement of the sleeping lord introduced at the beginning of the poem. Reference to the English, Anglo-French and Welsh names of Hay-on-Wye (*SL*, 94) again attests to the varied cultural components of Britain. The Welsh are referred to by the garrison as 'these broken dregs of Troea' (*SL*, 95), recalling once more the legend of the Trojan foundations of Britain. The poem ends with the question, 'Does the land wait the sleeping lord/ or is the wasted land/ that very lord who sleeps?' (*SL*, 96) This question encapsulates both the mythical expectations of the coming again of Arthur and other figures, which for Jones prefigure the Resurrection and the Second Coming,[37] and also the lament for nature ravaged by industrialization, and specifically the land of South Wales, a theme for which this poem stands out, although Jones' view that industrialization is inimical to artistic expression is found elsewhere in his work too. The idea that the land is the sleeping lord may also be meant as a type, to represent the religious understanding of the Church as the Body of Christ.

The last item in the collection is an extract from an abandoned project, *The Book of Balaam's Ass*, which Jones worked on between *In Parenthesis* and *The Anathemata*. The extract, reproduced as 'From *The Book of Balaam's Ass*', is included, as Jones explains in its preface, as representing 'a link of sorts' between his two major works (*SL*, 97). It starts with First World War stories told by veterans, and these slip into anecdotes about Roman campaigns in Britain. A section, which continues to the end of the extract, then describes an attempt by a British contingent to take a German machine-gun post during the First World War, concentrating on the ancestry of the various British and Irish soldiers, and the diverse ethnic components in their make-up (as well as listing the provenances of contingents who have previously failed to take the post): hardly anyone survives the assault, but the assorted relatives, beloveds and sacred figures called on are detailed. This allows Jones to introduce his vision of sacred history, with the New Testament crowning Hebrew and pagan Classical elements, and only sacred history, as Jones proposes, is capable of making sense of the slaughter. This fragment shows the concentration on the First World War of *In Parenthesis*, but makes more explicit the religious frame

---

37   For the parallel between Arthur and the Redeemer, see, for example, Pagnoulle, *David Jones: A Commentary*, 8. Xavier Baron, 'Medieval Arthurian Motifs in the Modernist Art and Poetry of David Jones', *Studies in Medievalism* 4 (1992), 253, points out that Jones' suggestion that the land of Wales is Arthur's body is characteristic of his sacramental thinking. See also Geraint Evans, 'Images of National Renewal', who sees the poem in terms of the values of national and cultural survival, and renewal.

which is further developed in *The Anathemata*. The recalling of the British Celtic, Gaelic Celtic, Anglo-Saxon, Nordic, Roman and other elements that go into making British culture and identity, and of British culture's connection to the wider European context, is present in both major works, and indeed is constant throughout the oeuvre.

David Jones, as we have seen, maintained a fairly constant set of concerns throughout his writing career, recombining them in various ways, highlighting different elements of his vision in different works, but seeking to include everything he saw as important every time. His approach of gathering in, with respect to art, also extends to national identity, so that his method, in understanding and describing a national identity, is one of inclusion, bringing together constituent ethnic groups, important historical events and features of the land. He does not talk about Britishness, but rather of things of the Island (of Britain), seeing these as including Welsh and English national identities, as well as Scottish, which he acknowledges, but talks less of, as he believes in writing about that of which he has personal experience and knowledge. No views as to what the political arrangements of his time ought to be are expressed. The Catholic perspective absolves him from the need to regard any given national identity as primary or absolute, since membership of, or relationship to, the Church is always of transcendent significance. Through the theory that only the good really exists, it also allows him to rehabilitate non-Catholic people and events from history, on the basis of the good that there is in them, and include all contributors in his vision of a complex weaving together of cultures with a supernatural purpose.

CHAPTER 2

Evelyn Waugh: The Material and the Spiritual

As is widely recognized, Evelyn Waugh's writing career divides into a first half, before the Second World War, consisting of satirical novels, with the satire sometimes bleak and biting even to the point of appearing nihilistic, and a second half, starting during the Second World War, when his work is characterized by a gentler, more reflective tone, and religious issues are often explicitly present (even though his conversion to Catholicism occurred during the first half, in 1930, when he was twenty-six).[1] Waugh's account of his ancestry in his partial autobiography *A Little Learning* will first be considered briefly together with the first book of his second career phase, *Brideshead Revisited*, in which the position of Catholics in England is a recurrent theme. The way the themes of national and religious identity feature in selected travel writings, and in his biography of the Catholic martyr, *Edmund Campion*, will be touched on, before turning to the detailed analysis of the late novels *Helena* and *Sword of Honour*, as these relate most closely to the works of David Jones and Muriel Spark discussed in this study. The autobiography provides a point of departure which presents the author's own national background, and signals its significance for the ensuing discussion of other works.

---

[1] Evelyn Waugh, *A Little Order: A Selection from his Journalism*, Donat Gallagher, ed. (London: Eyre Methuen, 1977), 145, 147.

A Little Learning

Waugh only wrote an autobiography of his early life. *A Little Learning*[2] covers his childhood, his university years at Oxford and his short spell of teaching at a boarding school in North Wales (which served as the basis for his early novel *Decline and Fall*), but does not reach as far as his conversion. In the first chapter, titled 'Heredity' (*LL*, 1–26), he gives a detailed analysis of his ethnic make-up by listing his eight great-great-grandfathers and their national origins. Of the eight, three were English, two Scottish, one Welsh, one Irish, and the remaining one English with a Huguenot inheritance. The descendants of all these great-great-grandfathers had however become English, and, although some of them had spent time in India, all the ancestors Waugh himself met were English. So, as he describes it, he had an unproblematic English identity, even if non-English elements could be discovered by genealogical investigation. There was also nothing in his background to encourage Catholic leanings, as he writes in 'Come Inside', a piece describing his conversion, but, rather, he claims, 'My family tree burgeons on every twig with Anglican clergymen' (*LL*, 147). Thus Waugh did not have the sense of division in his identity between ethnic groups that David Jones and Muriel Spark did, and his problematic of national identity is focused more exclusively on what makes Catholics in England separate from the rest of the population, as well as how English Catholics are part of an international Catholic community in a way which transcends, but does not cancel, their national identity. He does however appear to have a clear awareness of Welsh identity as separate from English, as seen for example in *Helena*, but this is not a major topic for him.

2   Evelyn Waugh, *A Little Learning* (London: Penguin, 1983) (*LL*). Further references to this edition are given after quotations in the text.

Travel Writing

Waugh's travel writing gives some clues as to his attitudes to religious and cultural identity, but his Catholic perspective does not become apparent until after *Labels*, his first travel book (1930); nevertheless his Catholic allegiance is discernible in his travel writings earlier than in his novels. *Brideshead Revisited* (1945) is the first novel in which Catholic themes appear openly.[3] The way that Waugh's religious allegiance affects his attitudes to national identity in his later travel writing, and especially in those works describing his travels in the Americas, merits attention. The works dealing with his travels in the Americas are especially interesting in connection with Waugh's approach to religious and national identity, as, in the context of Latin America, Catholic Hispanic civilization and mainly non-Catholic Anglo-Saxon civilization contrast, and sometimes come into conflict. Waugh's novel *A Handful of Dust* will be considered briefly too, in connection with his travel narrative on British Guiana, *Ninety-Two Days*,[4] as the material for the latter section of the novel derives from Waugh's British Guiana trip.

Waugh in the 1930s set off on distant expeditions – like many young writers of the time, as he points out in the preface to *When the Going was Good*, his 1946 selection from his previous travel writings.[5] His initial interests, like those of Graham Greene, Robert Byron and others, were to escape from the English ambience,[6] and to explore regions where, as he and

---

[3] This contrast between the relatively early appearance of overt Catholic themes in Waugh's travel writings, and their relatively late appearance in his novels, is noted by Martin Stannard, 'Debunking the Jungle: The Context of Evelyn Waugh's Travel Books: 1930–9', *Prose Studies* 5.1 (May 1982), 123.

[4] Evelyn Waugh, *Ninety-Two Days: Travels in Guiana and Brazil* (London: Serif, 2007) (*NTD*). Further references to this edition are given after quotations in the text.

[5] Evelyn Waugh, *When the Going was Good* (London: Penguin, 1951) (*WGG*), 8. Further references to this edition are given after quotations in the text.

[6] Valentine Cunningham, *British Writers of the Thirties* (Oxford: Oxford University Press, 1988), 377, among other critics, notes the escapist motivation of British writers travelling in the 1930s.

others saw it, civilization and its opposite met, as Lynda Prescott notes.⁷ Waugh's travel writing on the Americas complicated the 'civilization and barbarism' theme by adding to it the dimension of the meeting of Waugh's own Anglo-Celtic culture, which often appears, however, in a Protestant form, and a Latin culture, frequently embodying the Catholicism of his new religious loyalty. In addition, in Mexico, he confronts militantly secular forces in conflict with religion. These additional thematic focuses distinguish his American travel books from the other (post-*Labels*) travel books of his early Catholic years (his 1931 *Remote People* and his 1936 *Waugh in Abyssinia*, both set mainly in Africa, and especially in Ethiopia), such that his American travels force him to address his alignment in terms of Britishness and Catholicism more fundamentally than do his African travels.

Early in *Ninety-Two Days* Waugh signals that the theme of civilization and non-civilization will be prominent when, describing the varying stimuli for different types of authors he writes: '... for myself and many better than me, there is a fascination in distant and barbarous places, and particularly in the borderlands of conflicting cultures and states of development, where ideas, uprooted from their traditions, become oddly changed in transplantation' (*NTD*, 11). This self-diagnosis suggests that he is not only looking for a stark contrast between the civilized and an idea of the primitive, as Lynda Prescott believes Graham Greene is doing in his travel narratives *Journey Without Maps*, set in West Africa, and *The Lawless Roads*, set in Mexico.⁸ Rather, Waugh's interest is focused on the permutations that what he recognizes as civilization goes through when moved through space to a new environment, and it is also possible that he is seeking a clearer vision and understanding for himself of various types of European civilization by seeing them from an unfamiliar perspective. In British Guiana Waugh chose a peripheral part of the British Empire, one which would not have loomed largely in the British consciousness.

---

7   Lynda Prescott, 'Greene, Waugh and the Lure of Travel', *Books Without Borders, Volume 1: The Cross-National Dimension in Print Culture*, Robert Fraser and Mary Hammond, eds (Basingstoke: Palgrave, 2008), 152.
8   Ibid., 157.

Throughout *Ninety-Two Days* he compares what he sees in South America with British colonies in Africa, which he had visited on earlier journeys, and particularly emphasizes the lack of government in British Guiana: for example, the minimal 'Commissioner's residence' in Kurupukari, a single, unlocked, wooden building with nothing round it (*NTD*, 50–3), or the lack of any border crossing formalities on the border with Brazil (*NTD*, 92, 95). There is a minimal amount of British imperial control and administration to be seen. Moreover, he intended to make a significant part of his journey a river trip through Brazil, via Manaus, perhaps to contrast the British colony with a country which had been under Portuguese, and thus, continental European, Catholic, influence. In the event his plan does not come to fruition, and he gets no further into Brazil than the nearest town to the border, Boa Vista. In British Guiana, however, Brazilian influences are prominent, particularly in the plains region inland, such that he could be argued to be already partially in Latin America even before he crosses the border.

Boa Vista is presented as a disappointment, since it had been built up as a glamorous destination, praised by everyone Waugh came across on the way. However it is the scene of a failed development scheme, and is, at the time of Waugh's visit, torpid and plagued by violence. The unavailability of regular transport further into Brazil causes him to abandon his plan of seeing Manaus, and to return through British Guiana. So Waugh's experience of Boa Vista turns out not to be an advertisement for Latin civilization, which he does not travel far enough to reach, if it were there to be reached. On the other hand, Waugh plays with the idea of British civilization, in the absence of more than a scattering of people of mainly British origin, by comparing the native Indians with English people, and finding both groups very similar in character, thus subverting the idea that those furthest from European civilization will be most unlike the British, a notion which believers in British civilization might entertain: 'They like living with their own families at great distances from their neighbours ... they are unprogressive, unambitious, fond of pets, hunting and fishing ...' he notes of the indigenous Indians, among other similarities, which, on the English side, seem to apply especially to the country-house inhabiting section of society. Another ethnically non-English personage who can be seen as representing a subverted Englishness is the 'mystic' rancher Mr Christie, who is patriarch of his own private version of Christianity, including personal revelations, and whom Adam Piette[9] interprets as standing for the Calvinist principles which were a motive force in the establishment of the British Empire. What for the most part escapes satire is the network of Catholic hosts of various backgrounds, who give hospitality and help Waugh during his travels. These include the Harts, a Catholic ranching family, the father of which is American; the priest Father Mather at the St Ignatius Mission in Bon Success on the Brazilian border; Father Keary, who accompanies Waugh on part of the trip through the forest; and Father Alcuin, a German Benedictine in Brazil – Father Alcuin is lightly satirized, but is sympathetically treated, as are the other clergy in Boa Vista, in comparison with the city as a whole. Aside from a recovery from a dangerous situation which he attributes to a miracle (*NTD*, 130–2), Waugh tends to avoid overt Catholic apologetics in *Ninety-Two Days*. Nonetheless a glimpse of Waugh's notion of Catholic international civilization is offered in an understated way.

It has been widely noted that Waugh is one of the authors of the 1930s who reworked the same material on which they had written travel books to produce fiction, and Waugh's South American experiences, after forming the basis for *Ninety-Two Days*, played a significant role in his famous 1934 novel *A Handful of Dust*.[10] This novel satirizes its protagonist Tony Last's attachment to a philosophically vacuous vision of Englishness. It sees him set out in quest of a lost city in the South American jungle, which carries echoes both of the legendary cities sought by the first European explorers,[11]

---

9   Adam Piette, 'Travel Writing and the Imperial Subject in 1930s Prose: Waugh, Bowen, Smith, and Orwell', *Issues in Travel Writing: Empire, Spectacle, and Displacement*, Kristi Siegel, ed. (New York: Peter Lang, 2002).

10 For example, Helen Carr, 'Modernism and Travel (1880–1940)', *The Cambridge Companion to Travel Writing*, Peter Hulme and Tim Youngs, eds (Cambridge: Cambridge University Press, 2002), 74, notes this of Waugh as well as of Graham Greene, E. M. Forster and D. H. Lawrence.

11 Neil L. Whitehead, 'South America/Amazonia: The Forest of Marvels', *The Cambridge Companion to Travel Writing*, Peter Hulme and Tim Youngs, eds (Cambridge:

and of St Augustine's City of God.[12] He is however punished for his, as Waugh sees it, foundation-less romanticism, by being imprisoned in the jungle by a mad patriarchal semi-English figure, Mr Todd, a representative of a subverted Englishness, inspired by the real Mr Christie,[13] who forces him to read the works of Dickens aloud to him never-endingly (Waugh having found Dickens material to read himself during his British Guiana trip). Waugh seems to be suggesting that both versions of Englishness, Tony Last's, and Mr Todd's, are equally directionless and lacking in purpose. *A Handful of Dust* itself does nothing to suggest what this lacking purpose could be, but it might be hinted at in the novel's corresponding travel volume, *Ninety-Two Days*, in Waugh's apparent endorsement of his Catholic hosts.

Waugh was sponsored by an oil company to make the trip to Mexico on which his 1939 travel book *Robbery Under Law* is based.[14] His brief was to make the oil companies' case against their recent expropriation by the Mexican government. As Michael Brennan argues,[15] Waugh does this, but then moves on to tackle a subject more important to him, the Mexican government's persecution of the Catholic Church, a theme which dominates the book. *Robbery Under Law* is unusual as a travel book, in that it does not follow the author's itinerary, and in fact he does not seem to have had a particular itinerary, but rather to have stayed in Mexico City and made

---

Cambridge University Press, 2002), 147, believes that Raleigh set the tone for subsequent descriptions of British Amazonia, and that the idea of hidden cities is part of his legacy.

12 Peter Miles, 'The Writer at the Takutu River: Nature, Art, and Modernist Discourse in Evelyn Waugh's Travel Writing', *Studies in Travel Writing* 18, No. 1, 2004, 74–6, discusses the element of a quest for 'the City' in *Ninety-Two Days* with Boa Vista, on a material level, being the disillusioning target.

13 This link is widely recognized, as, for example, by Miles, 'The Writer at the Takutu River', 69.

14 Evelyn Waugh, *Robbery Under Law: The Mexican Object-Lesson* (Pleasantville, NY: Akadine, 1999) (*RUL*). Further references to this edition are given after quotations in the text.

15 Michael Brennan, 'Graham Greene, Evelyn Waugh and Mexico', *Renascence* 55.1 (Fall 2002).

excursions to investigate political conditions, particularly in relation to the treatment of the Church and the consequences of land reforms. The book is organized by theme, rather than by sequence of events during his stay, and while he tackles a series of potentially independent subjects, such as Mexican independence, the government expropriation of foreign oil companies operating in Mexico, Mexican anti-clericalism and the state of the Church, Mexico's relations to the United States, the Mexican government's six-year plan, and competition for influence over Mexico between the United States and Germany, he brings to bear a unified stance based on a view of Mexico as having deteriorated in terms of development since independence, of the persecution of the Church as being in large measure a cause of this deterioration, and of American intervention as partly responsible for the Church's persecution. Waugh had been a Catholic for eight years by the time he made his trip to Mexico, and his to a large extent disapproving attitude to American political influence in Mexico suggests he identified the Americans more as Protestants, and therefore antagonistic to the kind of Catholic society he now identifies himself with, than as fellow Anglo-Saxons and thus participants in the kind of English-based civilization he might otherwise have felt loyal to. In the face of popular English prejudices against Spanish culture Waugh is at pains to point out the high level of educational and economic development in pre-independence Mexico, and especially to emphasize its greater development in comparison with the British colonies, later the United States, to the north (for example *RUL*, 121–3), asserting, among other things, that three universities were founded in the Spanish American colonies almost a hundred years before the first British American university, and that anatomy and surgery were being taught by means of dissection in Mexico earlier than in England. Waugh appears particularly to enjoy discrediting stories told by various English-speakers about ecclesiastical abuses in Mexico, and places special emphasis on the role with which he credits the Mexican Church of transcending ethnic division in Mexico, by retelling the Guadalupe apparitions, in which the Virgin Mary appeared in the shape of an indigenous Indian, in support of his contention. Overall in *Robbery Under Law* Waugh appears neutral about ethnic groups as such but supportive of the Catholic Church as an international force promoting social cohesion and development, as Robert Murray Davis notes.[16] Unlike the subverted reproduction of a directionless Englishness which Waugh depicts in *A Handful of Dust*'s Mr Todd, based on British Guiana's Mr Christie, in *Robbery Under Law* Waugh hints at a successful replication of a Catholic civilization in Mexico, even if this later collapsed, partly through universal human weakness and partly through interventions, sometimes well intentioned and sometimes not, from the north.

The treatment of tensions between national and religious identities is less prominent in Waugh's travel writing on parts of the world other than Latin America. However, in the first of his two volumes on Ethiopia, *Remote People*,[17] he criticizes the Ethiopian Church for obscurantism comparing it unfavourably to the Western (Catholic) Church in this respect, and repeating this criticism in his second volume on Ethiopia, *Waugh in Abyssinia*,[18] where he finds that 'Compared with the manifestations of historic Christianity in any other part of the world, West or East, the decoration was shoddy, the ceremony slipshod, the scholarship meagre' (*WA*, 49). His conviction that the Western (Catholic) form of Christianity is more adequate may have contributed to his support for the Italian colonization of Ethiopia as expressed in *Waugh in Abyssinia*, although he follows his criticism of the Ethiopian Church with the contention that the indigenous modernizing movement in Ethiopia (Jeunesse d'Éthiopie) would in any case have curtailed the Church's influence, such that support for Ethiopia's independence need not follow, in his view, with a wish to preserve the Ethiopian Church's influence (*WA*, 49–50).

In Waugh's late African travel book *A Tourist in Africa*[19] he gives a glowing account of Genoa, where he sails from, and takes an interest in Catholic missionaries wherever he finds them on his travels, including

---

16   Robert Murray Davis, 'The Rhetoric of Mexican Travel: Greene and Waugh', *Renascence* 38.3 (Spring 1986), 167–8.
17   Evelyn Waugh, *Remote People* (London: Penguin, 2002).
18   Evelyn Waugh, *Waugh in Abyssinia* (London: Penguin, 1985) (*WA*). Further references to this edition are given after quotations in the text.
19   Evelyn Waugh, *A Tourist in Africa* (London: Methuen, 1985) (*TA*). Further references to this edition are given after quotations in the text.

providing a detailed description of a Catholic mission school in the then Rhodesia (*TA*, 125–32). He also notes and criticizes the racial theories of Cecil Rhodes, whom he regards as having been 'puerile' (*TA*, 151), especially noting his 'schoolboy's silly contempt' for 'the whole Mediterranean-Latin culture' (*TA*, 151) – that this prejudice is especially noteworthy and objectionable to Waugh is unsurprising given Waugh's self-identification with Catholic culture.

Overall, in Waugh's travel writing after *Labels*, a Catholic loyalty can be seen coexisting with his national loyalty, and sometimes taking precedence over it. His attachment to Catholic culture also makes him sympathetic to Catholic nationalities, particularly to Italians (an attitude which may have contributed to his making the protagonist of *Sword of Honour*, Guy Crouchback – who partially represents Waugh himself – a resident of Italy), but in the context of Latin America he is well disposed to Catholic Spanish- and Portuguese-speaking culture, and resents Protestant Anglo-Saxon (American) interference with it. He displays a detached attitude to British imperialism, not being against all manifestations of imperial activity, but at the same time failing to endorse, and even mocking, the kind of British imperialism which would see its justification in the idea of the superiority of Anglo-Saxon culture to all others.

Two Lives: Edmund Campion – Ronald Knox

Waugh's biography of the sixteenth-century English Catholic martyr Saint Edmund Campion, included in *Two Lives*,[20] was first published in 1935, and written between 1934 and 1935 (Edmund Campion was already beatified when the book was written, but not yet canonized). Campion was an Oxford academic who trained and worked as a priest and a Jesuit on

---

20   Evelyn Waugh, *Two Lives: Edmund Campion – Ronald Knox* (London: Continuum, 2001) (*TL*). Further references to this edition are given after quotations in the text.

the continent, in Douai, Rome, Brno and Prague, and later returned to England as part of the clandestine Jesuit Mission, but he was caught and martyred. While writing this biography can be seen as in itself a statement of Waugh's English and Catholic identity, of particular relevance for this study is the part of the narrative where Waugh describes the history of Prague just before Campion's arrival there as a Jesuit. He tells how the reformer Huss and his followers expelled foreign students from the university (these students went to Leipzig to found a university there), turning Prague from the centre of culture for Central Europe into a backwater. He claims that it is 'particularist sentiment' (*TL*, 43) that Huss appealed to, and that it was this same sentiment which was the mainstay of the reformers who followed him in the sixteenth century. As will be seen in the discussion of *Helena*, Waugh often makes comments about his time and place indirectly, when writing about other times and places, and it seems likely that in condemning Hussite particularist sentiment, and connecting this sentiment with Protestantism generally, through its founders, he is making an indirect criticism of the particularism of Protestant Anglo-Saxon culture, and mourning the loss of the international community, of which the Reformation has, as he sees it, deprived Britain.

Brideshead Revisited

Waugh's novel *Brideshead Revisited*,[21] written during 1944[22] (published in 1945), after Waugh had already been a soldier in the Second World War (and before a further deployment in Croatia), marks the introduction

---

21 Evelyn Waugh, *Brideshead Revisited* (London: Penguin, 1962) (*BR*). Further references to this edition are given after quotations in the text.
22 See Evelyn Waugh, *The Diaries of Evelyn Waugh*, Michael Davie, ed. (London: Penguin, 1979), 558–68.

of the Catholic theme into Waugh's work,[23] and although nationality is only a minor theme, there are several points at which the predicament of the English Catholic is highlighted, and this relates to the major theme, which is that of the divine as it works in what appears as a mainly secular world. The first-person narrator, Charles Ryder, gets to know an aristocratic English Catholic family through meeting its second son, Sebastian, while they are at university in Oxford. The first introduction of the family seat, Brideshead, in the novel presents it as superficially in every way an English country house like any other, but with the occasional sign of what to the non-Catholic reader (and, the narrative implies, to Charles) would be likely to seem incongruous and even exotic customs. For example, Sebastian takes Charles to see his old nanny in a remote part of the house, and among the decorations and furnishings of her room, 'There was a rocking horse in the corner and an oleograph of the Sacred Heart over the mantelpiece ...' (*BR*, 38). The nanny has a rosary in her hands when they find her asleep, and Sebastian genuflects when he shows Charles the chapel, even though he is barely practising as a Catholic when in Oxford. On a later visit, in response to the comment from Charles about Catholics that 'They seem just like other people' (*BR*, 87), Sebastian explains the predicament of English Catholics:

> My dear Charles, that's exactly what they're not – particularly in this country where they're so few ... they've got an entirely different outlook on life; everything they think important is different from other people. They try to hide it as much as they can but it comes out all the time. (*BR*, 87)

Sebastian's elder brother, Brideshead, reinforces the impression of this half-hidden but profound difference, by having a tendency to analyse situations in a scholastic manner, learnt at the Catholic school, Stonyhurst; the dramatic climax of the novel consists in Sebastian's sister Julia not marrying Charles, although they are in love, because she is already married and

---

23   As noted by James F. Carens, *The Satiric Art of Evelyn Waugh* (Seattle: University of Washington Press, 1966), 16, and Joseph Pearce, *Literary Converts: Spiritual Inspiration in an Age of Unbelief* (London: HarperCollins, 1999), 236.

cannot, from a Catholic point of view, divorce (this despite the fact that for most of the novel, like Sebastian, she is not observant). So, to the limited extent to which nationality is a theme in the novel, the point that emerges is that English Catholics have a fundamentally different set of values to that of the non-Catholic majority, but that members of the non-Catholic majority will fail to appreciate this difference on anything less than a close acquaintance with English Catholics.

Helena

Helena,[24] first published in 1950, though according to his diaries started on VE day in 1945,[25] is a short novel of Waugh's later period, relatively neglected by criticism.[26] It is Waugh's most explicitly religious novel, and one in which the issue of nationality is prominent. There are striking parallels with David Jones' world-view in the way in which Waugh makes the late Roman world stand for the contemporary British Empire, and even in the focus on Helena, an important and recurrent figure in Jones' literary universe.[27] The novel presents the life of the Empress Helena, starting with her meeting her husband Constantius while she is a princess in Britain. It then follows her journey through the Roman Empire to her husband's base in what is now Serbia; her life on the Dalmatian coast with her husband and her son, Constantine, and without her husband after he becomes

---

24 Evelyn Waugh, *Helena* (London: Penguin, 1963) (*Hel*). Further references to this edition are given after quotations in the text.
25 See *The Diaries of Evelyn Waugh*, 627.
26 Some critics regard *Helena* as unsuccessful artistically as a novel, for example A. A. De Vitis, *Roman Holiday: The Catholic Novels of Evelyn Waugh* (London: Vision Press, 1958), 66.
27 David Lodge, *Evelyn Waugh* (New York: Columbia University Press, 1971), 34–40, notes the implied parallel in *Helena* between the decline of late Roman Empire and what Waugh sees as the decline in twentieth-century civilization.

Emperor; her life in Trèves (Trier) after Constantine becomes Emperor; and her visit to Rome for Constantine's jubilee. It culminates in her journey to Jerusalem to find the True Cross, and her finding it there.

Waugh provides a preface (*Hel*, 9–11) which affords insight into his intentions in writing the novel. He explains that he has selected the legend according to which Helena was born in Britain, although he is well aware that another legend gives her place of birth as near Byzantium, because the British version suits his novelistic purposes, and he further recounts how when inventing details of the plot he has made them consistent with the few known facts about her (*Hel*, 9–10). During his explanation of this method he makes, as an aside, an important but indirect indication as to his intention in the novel: '... there is nothing, I believe, contrary to authentic history (save for certain wilful, obvious anachronisms which are introduced as a literary device)' (*Hel*, 9). He does not specify what the purpose of the devices is, but the notion of 'device' is suggestive of a purpose. The anachronisms are a prominent feature, especially in the early part of the novel, but to some extent throughout, and it is through them that the novel's possible interpretation as addressing twentieth-century issues can be understood.

The narrative starts, in the first section of Chapter 1, 'Court Memoir', with Helena as a teenage princess in Colchester, having *The Iliad* read to her in Latin by her tutor and slave, Marcias, while she distractedly looks out from the palace over the town, in the direction of the sea. Waugh mixes details which would still be true of Essex today with unfamiliar details of ancient life, and plays with Helena's national characteristics in ways which introduce ambiguities as to the senses in which she is 'British'. Already in the first sentence the day is set as 'the wet afternoon of the Nones of May' in the year 273 (*Hel*, 13), the wet spring day being something the contemporary British reader would recognize, but its description as 'Nones' being unfamiliar. The setting, the city of Colchester, still exists, but it is described as being the capital of the Trinovantes, whose chief is Coel, Helena's father (*Hel*, 13), the legendary figure mentioned often in David Jones' work. By using the Welsh spelling of Coel's name, rather than the English spelling 'Cole', Waugh shows an awareness of the Celtic identity this figure would have had; further hints at the idea of Welshness in connection with him occur later. Helena's red-haired colouring and tallness indicate Britishness, without particularly favouring English or Welsh associations – Waugh however indicates the historical gap by specifying that her looks are regarded as plain at the time, but would have been appreciated as beautiful in later periods (*Hel*, 13). Her attitude during her lesson, however, seems meant to bring to mind the English public school: 'the mood – at once resentful, abstracted and yet very remotely tinged with awe – of British youth in contact with the Classics' (*Hel*, 13). The word 'British' is potentially ambiguous here, as Helena is (Celtic) British (that is, Brythonic) ethnically, as well as being from Britain the island, but a modern school scene which is 'British' in the modern sense is also evoked. Coel's family is described as 'minor royalty' (*Hel*, 14) and Marcias explains to Helena that Britain is 'a young country' (*Hel*, 15), both circumstances likely to have been meant by Waugh to furnish an ironic contrast with the condition of the Britain of his contemporaries. The section includes an instance of the twentieth-century British slang which Helena often uses, when she describes the forthcoming banquet as 'tonight's beano' (*Hel*, 14). This kind of slang suggests a young upper-class person from England, so a type of person who might live in Colchester in Waugh's time. The section of *The Iliad* being read mentions Helen of Troy, and Helena is led to comment that 'Priam was a sort of relation of ours, you know' (*Hel*, 14). This statement relates to the myth of the Trojan foundation of Britain, often invoked by David Jones, and particularly associated with Welsh tradition, as Jones emphasizes. The link is perhaps made by Waugh as well, when Marcias comments that he has often heard this claim made by Helena's father, who is shown later as having a keen interest in ancestors, which Waugh seems to portray as a Celtic characteristic. However, an important function of this section is to introduce Helena's empirical leanings: in a discussion with Marcias she insists that the ruins of Troy must still exist, buried, and that she intends to discover them (*Hel*, 15). Helena's empirical inclination is what enables her to find the Cross later in the novel, but also invites interpretation as a 'British' characteristic.[28] The meaning of 'British' though, if this association

---

28 David Wykes, *Evelyn Waugh: A Literary Life* (Basingstoke: Macmillan, 1999), 162, sees Helena as a 'near caricature of a British empiricist'.

is made, is again open to question, as empiricism tends not to be popularly associated with Celtic culture, so is, rather, part of Helena's anachronistic 'English' identity, different from her father's 'Welsh' characteristics. In terms of philosophy, empirical tendencies might be said to appear in England in the Middle Ages (for example with Roger Bacon), but it would be difficult to trace an earlier presence. The idea that a British empiricist can be led to Catholicism by his or her empiricism is an important message of the book, and in conveying this message Helena is representing a twentieth-century British, or more specifically, English, person, rather than an ancient Briton. Hints of the fall of empires appear towards the end of the section, with Helena asking if Rome could ever be destroyed (*Hel*, 15) and mentioning the undignified fate of the Roman Emperor Valerian who has been captured by the Persians, and his stuffed body put on display (*Hel*, 16). Waugh, like Jones, is interested in civilizations in decline, and empires in dissolution.

In the first of the three short middle sections of the first chapter the parallel being drawn between the late Roman Empire and the late British Empire becomes more obvious, with Constantius (Helena and he will fall in love later that day), who is on a secret mission, and the District Commander, in the baths, having a military conversation about the state of the Empire and especially the state of its more problematic regions, an exchange which seems designed to bring to the reader's mind two twentieth-century British army officers discussing restive colonies. The District Commander comments, 'Shocking business about the Divine Valerian' (*Hel*, 17), using a mixture of colloquial English of the kind a twentieth-century British army officer might use and of the unfamiliar, to the reader, naming of the Emperor as divine, such that the third and twentieth centuries are co-present. One of Constantius' contributions to this conversation is, 'Yes, it's had the most disastrous effect on our prestige in the East' (*Hel*, 17). The expression 'the East' refers to the Persian-Mesopotamian frontier in the case of the Roman Empire, but reminds the reader of the eastern reaches of the British Empire. The reader is reminded again of the different status of Britain in the Roman Empire as compared with the British Empire, when Constantius brings up the issue of the morale of the 'frontier legions' (*Hel*, 18), such as the Second Augusta, a legion based in Britain, which was then at the frontier of the Empire. The same contrast is indicated when the District

Commander, explaining life in Britain to Constantius, tells him that 'We come under Gaul and we take our orders from there, provided they don't give us too many; when they do we just seem to forget about them' (*Hel*, 19). Britain is a subordinate and remote province, not the metropolis as in Waugh's time, but playing the role in Waugh's imagined Roman Empire that a far-flung but, for the time being, relatively tranquil outpost might in the British Empire of the mid-twentieth century.

The scene, in the following section, returns to Helena being read to about Paris and Helen, and the extract she hears evokes a burst of twentieth-century teenage British slang: 'What a lark! ... What a sell! ... Oh, what sucks!' (*Hel*, 20).[29] In this section Celtic background is suggested as part of materials of her imagination stemming from her childhood in the form of what appear to be druids ('those white-robed men of the sickle and the mistletoe', *Hel*, 21) – she tends to imagine the classical figure Longinus as one of the white-robed druid-like men – and the figure of the Pict as traditional enemy is brought in through the mention of her memories of stories of her nurse's father, killed fighting against them. So her modern linguistic traits here contrast with cultural elements which place her in the distant past, although substituting druids and Picts for similar figures could put the situation in any epoch. Meanwhile, in the next brief section, Constantius uses informal twentieth-century military language, with slight adjustments to indicate a Roman setting, to warn his second-in-command to keep the soldiers discreet about their provenance: 'Corporal Major, the men are to take down their regimental numerals immediately ... If I hear anyone's been talking, I'll confine the lot to barracks' (*Hel*, 21). There is of course a potential comedy in presenting Roman soldiers talking like the British army during the Second World War, but Waugh's aim, like Jones', in his insistence on this trope, is the establishing of the historical parallel which carries the work's covert message (rather overt in Jones' case).

The first chapter's important final section portrays the evening banquet held in honour of the visiting Constantius, during which Constantius

---

29 On Helena's use of modern slang see Douglas Lane Patey, *The Life of Evelyn Waugh: A Critical Biography* (Oxford: Blackwell, 1998), 294–5.

and Helena fall in love. The women actually eat separately from the men, their feast eliciting from Helena, again, a British twentieth-century young person's slang in its praise: 'What a spread! ... What a blow-out!' (*Hel*, 22). The description of the food Waugh imagines a Roman meal might have consisted of, including a distinctly non-twentieth-century pitcher of mead, is accompanied by another reminder that Britain at this time is a province, not the metropolis, or even one of the leading centres of the Empire: 'it [the food provided for the banquet] would not have done in Italy or Egypt but it was well-suited to the British ladies' tastes and circumstances' (*Hel*, 22). When the women are ready to rejoin the men for the evening's concert, further defamiliarizing, non-twentieth-century elements are again stressed, such as the ladies' having to wait because 'The gentlemen have just gone to be sick' (*Hel*, 22), and her father's three mistresses being part of the procession of ladies of the royal family into the hall. However, in narrating the concert and the king's presentation of the music to the Roman visitors, Waugh plays with the connection between ancient British and Welsh identity. The stereotypes of Welsh love of singing and love of ancestry are brought in as the choral music starts with 'the lament for my ancestors' (*Hel*, 23), as Coel explains, and Coel further offers to translate the best parts, as the singing is 'in our native tongue' (*Hel*, 23), which would have been the British language, ancestor language of Welsh. Connections between Welsh mythology and English literary heritage are made by Waugh, as the song of the ancestors recounts the foundation of Britain by Brutus, descendant of Aeneas, a legend particularly associated with the Welsh, but also known as part of English legend, and discussed in detail by David Jones – Coel's comment, however, that at that point in the story 'we have almost, you might say, reached modern times' (*Hel*, 23), reminds readers that the perspective is many centuries in the past compared with their own, thus the now distant past is much less distant. The Welsh-English connection is followed up by the mention in the ancestral song of further ancestors of Coel, legendary British kings who are part of Welsh folklore and the subject of plays by Shakespeare, thus prominent in the English literary canon: Cymbeline is mentioned by name (*Hel*, 25), and Lear is hinted at: 'One took doctored wine at the hands of his stepdaughter and ran horribly amok in the forest ...' (*Hel*, 23). Conflict between the Romans and the Britons is also commemorated in the song: Coel announces, 'They are singing of the flagellation of Boadicea ... rather a delicate subject to us Romans, but very dear to my simple people' (*Hel*, 24). Here Waugh captures the ambiguous position of Coel, the Romanized native leader, and this ambiguous position can be seen again when, at the end of the song, he explains, 'This is a very modern song ... it was written by the chief bard in my grandfather's day to commemorate the annihilation of the IX Legion' (*Hel*, 25), after which he 'rumbled with amusement' (*Hel*, 25) while ensconced in a toga 'which contrary to metropolitan fashion he always wore at table' (*Hel*, 25). It is unclear where the King's sympathies lie – they are probably divided – but his dress also reveals his imperfect Romanization. Again, the description of the song as 'modern' produces temporal defamiliarization in the reader, but the fact that there is only a remove of two generations between the semi-Romanized Coel and his grandfather, who would seem to have harboured anti-Roman sympathies, indicates that the harmonization of British and Roman loyalties taking place in Coel and his subjects may yet be incomplete. The expression 'chief bard' contributes to the Welsh-related allusions, as well as perhaps again hinting at the link between the Welsh legends and Shakespeare. At the same time, Waugh seems to be portraying the concert scene in such a way as to remind the reader of official events in British colonies during the twentieth century, involving local rulers and British officials, with the local rulers expressing divided loyalties in their choice of cultural entertainment – Britain in this novel, however, being the periphery rather than the centre.

In the second chapter, 'Fair Helen Forfeit', when Coel is persuaded to allow Helena to marry Constantius, he complains of her choosing a 'foreigner', despite conceding that 'we're all Roman citizens' (*Hel*, 31), and warns her, when she tells him that Constantius has promised to take her to 'The City' (Rome), that it's an '*Awful* place' (*Hel*, 31) and that 'No one goes there nowadays who can possibly help it – even the Divine Emperors' (*Hel*, 31). The whole conversation could be a twentieth-century British conversation simply by replacing 'Roman' with 'British', 'The City' with 'London', and 'the Divine Emperors' with 'the King' or 'the Royal Family'. The conflict expressed here is in Coel's sense that Roman citizens of other ethnicities are still foreign, and that parts of the Roman Empire outside

Britain are still abroad ('You won't like living abroad, you know', Coel tells Helena, *Hel*, 31), a conflict of identity that might have existed among citizens of the British Empire. Elsewhere in the chapter there is an emphasis on Helena's prowess in hunting and her knowledge of horses, stereotypically attributes of the aristocratic English young of the twentieth century, though some of her quarry (wild boar) puts her back in the third century, or at least well before the twentieth.

The third chapter, 'None but my Foe to be my Guide', starts with a description of the newly married couple's sea crossing from Britain to Gaul. Waugh again plays with contemporary echoes while reminding the reader that the action is taking place in antiquity. He calls the port they arrive at Boulogne, and describes it so as to make it recognizable to the many of his readers likely to have made the crossing themselves, with a high citadel towering over the harbour, but he makes sure that the details, such as the 'columned temple' (*Hel*, 37) at the top of the hill, in place of the prominent church – the Basilica of Notre Dame – now there, are classical. Perhaps there is play involving deliberate ambiguity, given the Basilica's neo-classical appearance. The port is 'so foreign', but also 'the gate to a new life', and 'the starting point of the road ... that led to Nish, to Rome, and whither beyond?' (*Hel*, 37). These hints as to her future direction of travel, in close conjunction with her sense of the Gaulish channel port as foreign, are significant, as in later life she loses the sense of the European continental lands of the Roman Empire as foreign.

The following episode, which involves a conversation between Helena and Constantius about the wall surrounding the Roman Empire, is crucial for the meaning of the novel. They are travelling eastwards through what is now Germany, along the border of the Empire, and there is a ditch and wooden wall along the frontier. The conversation starts with Helena asking whether there must always be a wall, a question the sense of which Constantius does not initially understand. However, he goes on to produce a panegyric on the wall, his imagination captured by the contrast between the order and industry on the inside, and the wildness on the outside, which is kept out. This is the meaning of 'The City' for him. Helen follows this with her own vision, one of Rome extending beyond the wall into the wider world. Constantius interprets what she says as meaning that she is talking about a further major expansion of the Roman Empire (which he believes impractical), but Helena insists that this is not what she has in mind: 'I didn't mean that. I meant couldn't the wall be at the limits of the world and all men, civilized and barbarian, have a share in The City?' (*Hel*, 40). Although not explicit (or yet understood by Helena herself) this vision of hers is a kind of prediction, and an assertion by Waugh of the continuity between the Church and the Roman Empire. A hint as to this being the significance of the vision lies in the way that Helena, mentioning peoples who Rome might extend to (and beyond) in the future, chooses ones who in fact were later Christianized (Germans, Ethiopians and Picts), and she also imagines further peoples 'beyond the ocean' (*Hel*, 39), a prediction, it would seem of, for example, the Church in the Americas. Waugh here is expressing the idea of the Church as a kind of new homeland, one which will transcend ethnicity, a point he will make more explicitly later in the novel.[30] The idea of the continuity between the Roman Empire and the Church, and of the Church as a kind of spiritualization of the Roman Empire, is important for David Jones too, as we have seen. The idea that something material can have a spiritual dimension, and that the spiritual dimension does not cancel or negate its material identity, is another key theme in the novel, which emerges more clearly in the later parts, but is already indicated here.

When they reach Ratisbon (Regensburg), Helena is left by Constantius for an extended stay of a couple of months, while he departs on mysterious business. This episode enables Waugh again to stress the strangeness of continental life to the uninitiated Helena, and her realization of the smallness and peripheral character of her places of origin. Ratisbon is the largest town she has yet seen, the Government House the largest house she has been in, and the Governor's wife, from Italy, considerably taller than her. She also finds that she cannot fully understand the local society ladies' 'rapid, allusive Latin' (*Hel*, 42). In Ratisbon Helena also becomes aware of mystery cults from the East being followed, a theme which has

---

30 Ian Littlewood, *The Writings of Evelyn Waugh* (Oxford: Blackwell, 1983), 116, sees this passage as marking the transition from the romantic to the religious viewpoint.

already been lightly hinted at through the interest of Marcias, her tutor, in esoteric matters, and his desire to move to Alexandria to pursue them. Helena here, as always, reacts with her anachronistic British empiricism, telling the Governor's wife, on the subject of the mystery cults, 'It's all bosh, isn't it?', a favourite phrase of hers (*Hel*, 43).

Helena and Constantius arrive at their destination, Constantius' home town Nish, now in Serbia, at the end of the third chapter, and this is where Constantine is born, but during Constantine's childhood the family moves to Dalmatia, and it is there that Constantine grows up, and where Helena is when Constantius becomes Emperor and divorces her, and where she waits for Constantine to return after his education and training. It is notable that Nish is presented as a disagreeable place, with boorish inhabitants ('Helena found none to love among them; they were a prosaic race', *Hel*, 50), whereas the Dalmatian coast is beautiful, and the inhabitants are 'genial' (*Hel*, 58). There is a memorable description of the family's journey through the frigid upland landscape just before they reach the slopes down to the coast, and the moment when the ice disappears and a spring landscape appears to Helena, including 'vineyards and olive groves and orchards' and 'a rich landscape of villas and temples and little walled towns' (*Hel*, 58). While there is no doubt that Waugh's descriptions of these places are based on his own experiences during his mission to Yugoslavia during the Second World War (these experiences are also the basis for an important section of *Sword of Honour*), and while the Dalmatian coast has undeniable climatic advantages over the interior, the contrast between the paradise-like portrayal of Dalmatia and the negative picture of Nish, including the inhabitants, would seem to constitute a projecting back of his own preferences, and perhaps prejudices, onto Helena's world. However, this may not be accidental, as a theme of the novel which emerges in its latter part is the division between the Eastern and Western churches, a conflict which Waugh represents, consistently with his strategy throughout the novel, partly historically and partly anachronistically, projecting modern elements of the Catholic-Eastern Orthodox division back onto Helena's time. Given that his presentation of the conflict is unashamedly pro-Western and pro-Catholic, it is perhaps not surprising that Waugh here favours the Catholic over the Orthodox part of what was in his time Yugoslavia. In a similar way, it is arguably significant that the parts of Europe where Helena settles happily, where she is content enough to consider staying permanently (for example in Dalmatia, 'Now I've struck root here, emperors or no emperors', *Hel*, 72), and not to be tempted by the idea of moving back to Britain, even though she is free to do this after her divorce from Constantius, are Dalmatia, Trèves (Trier) and Rome, all in Waugh's time part of Catholic Europe. While Helena gains a Roman as well as a Christian identity during the course of the novel, which allows her to feel at home in locations which earlier she would have felt as foreign, nevertheless in her role as representing Waugh himself, a role indicated towards the end of the novel, as we shall see below, she may also be expressing Waugh's own sense of where he feels at home due to his Catholic identity. This indication as to Waugh's own attitudes connects with his portrayal of the hero of *Sword of Honour*, Guy Crouchback, as in some ways more at home in Italy than in Britain.

Trèves, now in Western Germany, is the setting of the sixth chapter, 'Ancien Régime', and Helena is taken there by her son Constantine, who leaves her there when he becomes Emperor. It is one of the places where she settles and feels at home: 'It was an enchanting place, with all the opulence and chic of Milan sharpened by a Northern tang of its own which Helena recognised and loved' (*Hel*, 78). It is also the scene of her conversion to Christianity, but, before that, of an important encounter, between her and her old tutor Marcias, which shows Helena's empiricist disposition. We may first look back to a similar scene from Chapter 4, in which a conversation occurs between Constantius and Helena, in which Helena asks Constantius about the Mithraic cult he has joined. Helena listens to him recounting the foundation myth, but then disturbs him by asking him where it happened, and when, and how he knows. Constantius interprets these questions as 'childish' (*Hel*, 66) and irreverent (*Hel*, 67), and she does not receive any answers. In Trèves, Helena attends a lecture on gnosticism, only to recognize the lecturer as Marcias, who has now become a famous authority. After the lecture she asks Marcias the same questions about the Gnostic myth that she asked Constantius about the Mithraic myth: 'When and where did all this happen? And how do you know?' (*Hel*, 83). Marcias later tells her that she had asked 'a child's question' (*Hel*, 84). He also dismisses the possibility of a less esoteric religion flourishing at that period, saying 'We live in a very old world today' (*Hel*, 84). While Helena's empiricist leaning is part of her anachronistic Britishness, Marcias' description of the world of the late Roman Empire as old has implications for Waugh's view of his own time:[31] high modernity is also a time of a proliferation of esoteric sects, a tendency Chesterton is famous for highlighting and mocking. On the evening of the day of the lecture, Helena talks to a poet friend of hers, Lactantius, and first remarks on the lecture on gnosticism, 'It's all bosh, isn't it?' (*Hel*, 84), and then asks him similar questions on Christianity to the ones she had posed about the mystery religions. Lactantius is able to give her some literal answers as to times, places and how he knows: while this conversation is not explicitly connected by Waugh to her subsequent conversion, it seems to indicate that belief in Christianity is possible for someone of an empirical, and therefore (modern) British, disposition.

During the next (seventh) chapter Constantine wins the battle at the Milvian Bridge, and starts to protect the Church. After this, Helena is converted, though the conversion itself is not described in detail; and when she is beyond the age of seventy, and not expecting to leave Trèves, she is invited to Rome by Constantine for his jubilee, an invitation she unexpectedly accepts, although the reader is not taken by surprise, knowing that going to Rome was a girlhood ambition. Chapter 8, 'Constantine's Great Treat', and Chapter 9, 'Recessional', narrate her time in Rome, the third of the locations in Europe where she feels at home and seems likely to settle permanently. Early in Chapter 8, and during her stay in Rome, there comes a statement of her altered sense of her relationship to other people since joining the Church (perhaps reflecting a similar experience on Waugh's part): a new sense of identity and belonging, which transcends ethnic categories. Earlier she had disliked crowds, but now,

---

31 See George McCartney, 'Helena in Room 101: The Sum of Truth in Waugh and Orwell', *Waugh Without End: New Trend in Evelyn Waugh Studies*, Carlos Villar Flor and Robert Murray Davis, eds (Bern: Peter Lang, 2005), 67, for the point that Helena's rejection of mystery cults can be compared with Waugh's own rejection of the mystifications he saw as characteristic of modern thought.

> She was in Rome as a pilgrim and she was surrounded by friends. There was no way of telling them. There was nothing in their faces. A Thracian or a Teuton might stop a fellow countryman in the streets, embrace him and speak of home in his own language. Not so Helena and the Christians. The intimate family circle of which she was a member bore no mark of kinship. The barrow-man grilling his garlic sausages in the gutter, the fuller behind his reeking public pots, the lawyer or the lawyer's clerk, might each and all be one with the Empress Dowager in the Mystical Body. And the abounding heathen might at any hour become one with them. There was no mob, only a vast multitude of souls, clothed in a vast variety of body, milling about in the Holy City, in the See of Peter. (*Hel*, 93)

This key passage shows how the supranational identity which Helena acquires through the Church is a kind of spiritual counterpart of the identity Helena had as a Roman citizen, although, as the passage indicates, the Christian identity is open to all, whereas Constantius' understanding of the significance of the Roman Empire was of something which would always divide the world into Roman and non-Roman, hence the need for walls. Waugh makes it clear here that he is talking about the Catholic Church by using terms such as the See of Peter and the mystical body. Thus the passage may reflect something of his own feelings after his conversion on travelling inside and outside the British Empire, and his perspective on the people he meets. Helena here is not shown seeking out fellow Britons, as the passage hints she might have. A tendency to look for centres of Catholicism rather than fellow Britons while on his travels is arguably discernible in Waugh's travel writing, as, for example, in *Ninety-Two Days*.

Later in Chapter 8 Helena again shows her sceptical common sense by failing to be impressed by Eusebius, the charming but exiled Bishop of Nicomedia, who is shown as having unorthodox leanings, and who reminds Helena of her tutor, Marcias (*Hel*, 98–9). Although this episode can partly be interpreted in the light of Waugh's preoccupation with what he sees as a tendency to obscurantism in Eastern Christianity, Eusebius' urbane manner and concern with keeping up with the times might in fact, in view of the Roman Empire-British Empire parallel running through the novel, represent Waugh's vision of an Anglican clergyman – at home with the political establishment but vague on doctrine. In Chapter 9 Helena, in the same hard-headed vein, is sceptical about the military standard

Constantine shows her, which he claims to have been his standard at the Milvian Bridge, even though it is elaborately ornamented with Christian symbols, which could not have been done, Helena observes, between the night before, when Constantine had his vision relating to Christianity, and the day of the battle (*Hel*, 124). Later Constantine tells Helena and Pope Sylvester that he will move the capital to the East, and build a new centre for Christendom focused on two churches dedicated to Wisdom and Peace, thus avoiding the 'unpleasant associations' (*Hel*, 125) that Rome has owing to the presence there of the bones of martyrs, including Peter and Paul. In conversation without Constantine (who has left Rome by this time), Helena and Sylvester are agreed in their opposition to Constantine's concept. Sylvester expresses the view, 'Unpleasant associations are the seed of the Church' (*Hel*, 126), while Helena puts her opinion in more detail: 'You can't just send for Peace and Wisdom, can you? ... and build houses for them and shut them in. Why, they don't exist at all except *in people*, do they? Give me real bones, every time' (*Hel*, 126). Just before this statement Helena has claimed that her dislike of the New Rome is connected to people in the country she comes from not liking new things (*Hel*, 126). Helena is showing her British empirical mindset in a way which, perhaps unexpectedly, supports the Catholic veneration for relics, and also hints at the special task she is going to perform, to find the True Cross (she makes the decision to go in search of it later in the same exchange). Waugh's theme that every person is meant for a providentially ordained task, which no one else can perform, is hinted at, and it is Helena's (anachronistic) Britishness which is part of what makes her the person to perform the task of finding the Cross.[32] In addition, her speech here highlights the philosophical-theological theme of the novel, that the physical and spiritual worlds are both real, and interact. Helena's warm relationship with Pope Sylvester, and their shared scepticism about tall stories, such as sacred cities in the

---

32   Donat Gallagher, 'The Humanizing Factor: Evelyn Waugh's "Very Personal View of Providence"', in Flor and Murray, eds, *Waugh Without End*, 25, stresses how, from the point of view of the novel, finding the Cross is the specific extra task that God wants from Helena.

East, and a miracle that Sylvester himself is believed to have performed, could be part of Waugh's attempt to convince his compatriots that Roman (Catholic) and British mindsets are not incompatible.[33]

Helena departs for Aelia Capitolina (Jerusalem) in 326 (at the beginning of Chapter 10), starting from Nicomedia, near Constantinople. Once there (Chapter 11, 'Epiphany'), lodging with the nuns at Mount Zion (an anachronistic hint, it would seem, of the nuns resident there in Waugh's time, and today), Helena sets out on her quest to find the Cross, ordering some basilicas to be founded while she searches. During enquiries she makes of people in the area who might have expertise shedding light on the Cross, what it was made of, and what could have happened to it, Waugh again shows her sceptical nature at work, rejecting fanciful symbolic stories offered to her by clergymen who are mainly Copts, about what woods the Cross was made of (*Hel*, 140–1). The Copts stand here for what Waugh sees as the obscurantism of the Eastern Churches, an obscurantism which he elsewhere criticizes in relation to the Ethiopian Church (which is closely allied with the Coptic Church). In *Remote People*, one of two travel books on Ethiopia, in response to witnessing the Ethiopian liturgy at the monastery of Debra Libanos, he praises the Roman liturgy for the fact that the sanctuary remains open to view, whereas the Ethiopian sanctuary is veiled during the liturgy.[34] Waugh is likely to have singled out the Copts here because they are associated with the doctrine of Monophysitism, which in its extreme form claims that Jesus has only a divine nature, not a human nature, while Waugh is advocating the crucial significance of both the physical and spiritual realms. Waugh has an Italian clergyman present, who takes a drily practical view, objecting to the idea that vegetable life needs to be redeemed – the suggestion here appears to be that British Helena and the Roman Church are equally hard-headed, and equally committed to a practical as well as a spiritual position. Chapter 11 ends with the significant

---

33 See Robert Murray Davis, *Evelyn Waugh, Writer* (Norman, Oklahoma: Pilgrim Books, 1981) for a discussion of the contrast between the real Rome and the unreal projected holy Eastern city.

34 This passage is discussed in Robert Murray Davis, *Evelyn Waugh and the Forms of his Time* (Washington, DC: Catholic University Press of America, 1989), 161–3.

scene in which Helena goes to celebrate Epiphany at Bethlehem, and utters a long prayer to the Three Kings, including these lines: 'You are my especial patrons ... and patrons of all late-comers, of all who have a tedious journey to make to the truth ... of all who stand in danger by reason of their talents' (*Hel*, 145). As well as Helena making the connection between herself and the Magi, Waugh seems to be making the connection between himself and Helena. He is also a latecomer, as a convert, possibly in danger by reason of his talents, and the Magis' 'strange gifts' (*Hel*, 145), which Helena mentions, and which were accepted though not needed (*Hel*, 145), might correspond to Waugh's strange gift, this novel.[35] Helena actually finds the Cross in the twelfth and final chapter, returns as far as Constantinople, where Constantine now is, and dies soon afterwards, having insisted that she is to be buried in Rome.

A clue to the purpose and meaning of the novel is to be found in one of the last sentences, which begins, 'Britain for a time became Christian ...' (*Hel*, 158). The startling implication is, of course, that Britain is no longer Christian in his time. There is no explanation as to whether he means that it has not been Christian since the time it has not been Catholic, or whether he means that anything like orthodox Christianity has become uncommon in his time, replaced by various secular world-views, including materialism and non-religious spiritualisms. Although in this novel Waugh represents vague confusing ideas and mysticisms as coming from the East, nevertheless, given the suggestions throughout the novel that he has something to say about contemporary society, the novel's mystagogues and smooth-talkers can be taken to represent what Waugh sees as prominent presences in modern Britain. Waugh's thesis is that Catholicism, with its practical attitude to the realities of both the physical and spiritual realms, shares more common ground with those exhibiting a British empirical temperament than they themselves realize. He proposes to his compatriots in this novel that British and Catholic identities are compatible, that the

---

[35] Ma Eulàlia Carceller Guillamet, 'Religion and Reconciliation in *Helena*', in Flor and Murray, eds, *Waugh Without End*, 240, 220–1, discusses the parallels between Waugh and Helena as converts and latecomers.

sceptical attitude is at least part of what makes up the Catholic spirit (and is perhaps potentially the special British contribution), and recommends the recognition that the physical and spiritual realms are both real as the most genuinely hard-headed empirical attitude. It is worth mentioning that this book may also be a kind of act of reparation for the anti-Christian writing of a countryman, Gibbon, alluded to indirectly but unmistakably in Chapter 8, when the poet Lactantius, pointing to a pet gibbon, remarks, 'A man like that might make it his business to write down the martyrs and excuse the persecutors. He might be refuted again and again but what he wrote would remain in people's minds when the refutations were quite forgotten. That is what style does ...' (*Hel*, 80).[36]

Helena, then, is a novel which both argues for the potential compatibility of British identity with Catholic identity, but also suggests that once Catholic identity is acquired, it does not negate British identity but does override it. Helena remembers Britain from time to time in the course of the novel, remains British in her sceptical, no-nonsense temperament, but asks to be buried in Rome, and in later life shows a sense of especial kinship with members of the Church, rather than with fellow Britons, whom she shows no signs of seeking out.

Sword of Honour

Waugh's longest novel, *Sword of Honour* (first published in 1965)[37] results from the merging of what were originally published as three separate novels, *Men at Arms*, *Officers and Gentlemen* and *Unconditional Surrender*, which were nevertheless always intended to form a whole, as Waugh affirms in

---

36 Wykes, *Evelyn Waugh*, 158–65, points out that Waugh in *Helena* is trying to defeat Gibbon.
37 Evelyn Waugh, *Sword of Honour* (London: Penguin, 1999) (*SH*). Further references to this edition are given after quotations in the text.

the preface to *Sword of Honour* (*SH*, xxxiv). As he started the project in 1951,[38] its beginnings immediately postdate the publication of *Helena*. There are many shared concerns between the two books, but a few episodes will be picked out here which bear on Waugh's attitudes to Britishness and Catholicism, episodes which continue themes introduced in *Helena*, and even in *Brideshead Revisited*. *Sword of Honour* is a Second World War novel, and recounts the experiences through the whole war of the fictional protagonist, Guy Crouchback. Crouchback's experiences parallel Waugh's own fairly closely, but with some significant differences.[39]

Guy Crouchback is an English Catholic, like Waugh, but unlike Waugh is not a convert but a member of the recusant aristocracy. The novel opens with Guy about to leave the Italian town where his family have a holiday home in order to join the army in Britain, now that war seems inevitable. One of the themes of the novel is Guy's sense of estrangement from Britain, which he seems to overcome by the end of the novel. This estrangement has been acute during the time leading up to his departure from Italy just before the beginning of the war. Guy is thirty-five, and has been living at the house in Italy after a failed marriage combined with an attempt to settle in Kenya. His family seat in England has been rented to nuns, and there is no male heir in the family.

The house in Italy is the scene of 'Guy's happiest holidays with his brothers and sister' (*SH*, 3), as well as of his honeymoon. His being settled there is echoed by the presence of the tomb of a medieval English knight in the village's parish church, a knight who was held up on his way to the Crusades and never reached Palestine (a failure perhaps suggestive of Guy's being stranded without achieving his destiny, at this stage), and who is known locally as 'il Santo Inglese' (*SH*, 5) – Guy is shown visiting this tomb just before he leaves, on his own Crusade, and his visit to confession at the same time reminds the reader that he is, from a religious point of view, at one with the local Italian community in a way he would

---

38 See Angus Calder, Introduction, *SH*, xvii.
39 For an account of Waugh's own experiences during the Second World War see Calder's Introduction, *SH*, vii–xxviii, or Waugh's *Diaries*.

not be in England. However, Waugh describes Guy as being in a state of spiritual 'paralysis' (*SH*, 6) since his divorce. There are also hints at limits in the extent to which he is more at home in Italy than in Britain: he is not especially popular in the village, not considered as '*simpatico*' (*SH*, 7); as far as his Italian goes, 'He spoke the language well but without nuances' (*SH*, 6); and he looks (in Italy) 'plainly foreign but not so plainly English' (*SH*, 4). His feeling of being at home in Italy is incomplete, but the obstacle is a spiritual dryness, a lack of love generally. Waugh describes Guy's learning of the approach of war as 'first satisfaction' of a 'frustrated love' (*SH*, 3), a love for England. From Guy's point of view Britain has happened to find itself on the right side in the war, a war which offers him the possibility of fighting, as he sees it, 'the Modern Age in arms' (*SH*, 4), and this chance for him to fight with his countrymen in a war worth fighting has 'brought deep peace to one English heart' (*SH*, 4). Thus at the beginning of the novel, Guy's affinity for Italy, while real, and contributed to by his being able to take part there in the majority religious culture, has not effaced his need to express his sense of English identity in some way, an opportunity offered to him by political events. However, at the same time, it is already hinted that his malaise is not at a deeper level one of split national identity, but more importantly a spiritual alienation, a failure to come out of himself towards other people generally, and this failure is also one which historical circumstances are offering him a chance to address.

The relation of Guy's Catholicism to his Britishness is an important but background issue in *Sword of Honour*, and much of the novel is taken up by his various wartime experiences, his initial enthusiasm for and later disillusionment with his regiment, the 'Halberdiers' (a fictional regiment),[40] his disappointment when Communist Russia becomes an ally rather than an enemy, his deployments in Crete and Yugoslavia, and long periods of training. Also important is his personal life, especially his relationship

---

40   According to William J. Cook, *Masks, Modes and Morals: The Art of Evelyn Waugh* (Rutherford, NJ: Fairleigh Dickinson University Press, 1971), 270, Guy comes to realize that the Halberdiers are 'foreign' to him, in the sense of not sharing his convictions about right and wrong.

with his ex-wife Virginia, whom he eventually remarries, and with his father, a model of saintliness in the novel. Guy's Italian connections occasionally cause him to be viewed with suspicion in the army, for example, by Colonel Ritchie-Hook, who remarks, not recognising Guy as the man in question: 'There's one wretched fellow on my list spent half his life in Italy. I didn't care for the sound of that much' (*SH*, 57). He maintains his Catholic practices throughout the war, and comes into contact with various priests of different nationalities. Some of these contacts are not altogether felicitous, as is the case with an Irish priest at a seaside town he has to take the Catholic men of the regiment to, who is not a strong sympathizer with the Allied cause (*SH*, 50–1). More seriously, he encounters a priest in Egypt, whom he suspects of being a spy (and he turns out to be one), because extra questions the priest asks him in confession (*SH*, 327). However an incident late in the novel is significant in terms of his Catholic identity and resonates with themes in *Helena*. Guy, stationed on the Dalmatian coast as a part of a mission to liaise with the partisans, has recently learned that his wife has been killed in an air raid in London. He meets the local priest to ask him to say a Mass for his wife. There is a nervous atmosphere, as the partisans and the priest are suspicious of each other, and there is also a potential linguistic barrier between Guy and the priest, but Guy finds that they can communicate in Latin and makes the arrangement in a simple Latin conversation (*SH*, 623). This brief communication represents Guy and the priest both sharing a Catholic identity, partly because what they are talking about is only intelligible to Catholics, and is in fact misinterpreted by the partisans, who believe that they were carrying out some kind of espionage. The fact that the two men speak in Latin, the Church's language, also signifies the existence of something akin to a national identity, which is in fact a super-national identity. There are echoes of the old identity of the Roman Empire, and a reader of *Helena* may be reminded of Helena's ability to communicate with the inhabitants of the various places in which she lived in the Empire (including Dalmatia) in Latin. However, as we have seen, Helena also foresaw the expanding of Romanness beyond the boundaries of the Empire. Guy in *Sword of Honour* appears at home in Catholic Europe, an area which corresponds closely to the Western Roman Empire (without North Africa), but it is also clear that he can find minority Catholic communities wherever he goes, such that his Catholic identity cannot primarily be geographically defined. The anomaly is perhaps also hinted at, in *Helena* and *Sword of Honour*, that England and Wales, having constituted an important part of the Western Roman Empire, are not (in modern times) part of Catholic Europe.

Sword of Honour ends with Guy, after the war, returning to the family estate, taking over the running of the farm, settling in 'the agent's house' (because the main house is occupied by the nuns), and marrying an eligible Catholic woman – in addition he looks after the son, by another man, of his former wife, as his own son, and no more children are forthcoming (*SH*, 662–3). He sells the house in Italy. This ending represents a reconciliation (at least partial) of Guy with his Britishness. He has learned to accept imperfections, in others and in himself, during the war, so that a perfect spiritual understanding between himself and his compatriots is no longer necessary for him to live among them. His adoption of his wife's son by another man also seems to indicate that he has overcome his difficulty in loving, described at the beginning of the novel, and has put generosity above other, such as genealogical, considerations.[41] The continuity of the old Catholic family's spiritual traditions appears to be more important here than whether the continuer is genetically descended from the family.

Both *Helena* and *Sword of Honour* show personal identity as a journey rather than a static condition, and reconciliation of conflicting elements of identity is realized by seeing the elements as contributory factors to a movement of development and accumulation. *Helena* emphasizes two levels of reality, the physical-worldly and the spiritual, and their complementarity. From this point of view there is no need for, for example, an English identity and a Catholic identity to clash, as they operate at different levels of reality, the worldly identity or identities forming a necessary foundation in the journey towards the spiritual. *Helena* closely recalls David Jones' vision, in its portrayal of the way that an accumulation of cultural influences leads

---

41 William Myers, *Evelyn Waugh and the Problem of Evil* (London: Faber, 1991), 107, suggests that it is Guy's vocation to become the child's foster father (each character finding his or her vocation being an important motif in Waugh's novels).

to spiritual discovery, in *Helena* for an individual person (Helena herself), whereas in David Jones' works the focus is more on the development of a cultural community in this direction. In *Sword of Honour* another consideration comes to the fore: it is the person's orientation outwards from the self which allows development and reconciliation of inner divisions. The process is love, rather than a journey, although the journey metaphor is still applicable. While self-absorbed, Guy can feel at home with neither the British nor the Italian parts of his make-up, and even his Catholicism is portrayed as mechanical rather than fulfilling at the beginning of the novel. His move out of the self towards others allows him to escape from his impasse, and his acceptance of imperfection in others and in himself means that he can view the various elements of his background, despite imperfections, as stepping stones on his route to a perfection not yet achieved. The theme of the overcoming of inner personal identity conflicts through an outward orientation in love links *Sword of Honour* with Muriel Spark's novel *The Mandelbaum Gate*, which was first published in the same year, 1965, as the one-volume version of *Sword of Honour*.

CHAPTER 3

Muriel Spark: Layers of Identity

Muriel Spark was born in 1918 in Edinburgh, and she started her writing career as a poet. She began writing novels in the 1950s (having worked in publishing in London and in intelligence during the Second World War), after returning from Rhodesia (now Zimbabwe), where she had gone with her husband after an early marriage which proved to be short-lived.[1] Her first novel, *The Comforters*, published in 1957, based partly on her experience of a nervous breakdown, shows striking similarities with Evelyn Waugh's novel published in the same year, *The Ordeal of Gilbert Pinfold*, which was based on his nervous breakdown.[2] She became a Catholic in 1954, a move strongly influenced by her reading of Newman, as she recounts herself (*Curriculum Vitae*, 202–3, 'My Conversion', 24). In her fiction Spark cultivated a dry style, in which supernatural realities sometimes erupt into the everyday world, or are hinted at, but are always described in a non-emotional way, in order to present natural and supernatural realities as equally real. Although her works often have a protagonist who carries many of her own characteristics, and the plots are frequently partly autobiographical, the issue of the interaction between the national and religious identities of the protagonist is not generally highlighted as a prominent theme. The one novel in which this issue does feature as the leading theme

---

1   Information on Spark's earlier life can be found in her own *Curriculum Vitae: A Volume of Autobiography* (London: Penguin, 1993) (*CV*). Further references to this edition are given after the quotations in the text. Information on her life generally can be found in Martin Stannard, *Muriel Spark: The Biography* (London: Weidenfeld and Nicholson, 2009).
2   Spark discusses this episode in *CV*, 207–8.

is *The Mandelbaum Gate*,³ and this will be discussed here together with the short story, 'The Gentile Jewesses',⁴ which thematizes Spark's religious identity against the background of her family. In addition passages in her autobiography, *Curriculum Vitae*, which shed light on her attitudes to her national and religious identities, will be considered. Her most famous novel *The Prime of Miss Jean Brodie*⁵ also has passages which relate to religious and national identity, and which reinforce points Spark makes in *Curriculum Vitae* about her experience of growing up in Edinburgh. In Spark's case, the dimensions in which conflict of identity can occur include that of the relationship between Scottishness, Englishness and Britishness, and that of her Jewish identity – the extent to which she views herself as having been Jewish before her conversion to Catholicism, and whether she can still consider herself to be at least partially Jewish afterwards, constitute possible areas of conflict.

Curriculum Vitae

Although *Curriculum Vitae* (first published in 1992) was written after *The Mandelbaum Gate* and 'The Gentile Jewesses', it will be convenient to address it first in order to provide biographical foreground to the other works to be discussed. *Curriculum Vitae*, like Waugh's *A Little Learning*, is a fragmentary autobiography, dealing only with her early life. It covers her childhood in interwar Edinburgh, and moves on to describe her unsuccessful marriage in southern Africa, for which she left her home in Edinburgh

3   Muriel Spark, *The Mandelbaum Gate* (London: Penguin, 1967) (*MG*). Further references to this edition are given after the quotations in the text.
4   'The Gentile Jewesses', in Muriel Spark, *The Complete Short Stories* (London: Penguin, 2002) (GJ). Further references to this story in this edition are given after the quotations in the text.
5   Muriel Spark, *The Prime of Miss Jean Brodie* (London: Penguin, 1965) (*PMJB*). Further references to this edition are given after the quotations in the text.

in 1937, her return to war-time London and her work in an intelligence unit near London. It continues through her subsequent period working at a series of jobs in publishing and related activities, leading up to the beginning of her success with the publication of her first novel (*The Comforters*) three years after her conversion, but finishes there. *Curriculum Vitae* says very little about Catholicism, as her conversion happens close to the end of the book, but it sheds light on her mixed Scottish, English and Jewish background, as well as making a theme of Scottish-English relations in the early parts of the book. She was particularly aware of the issue of Scottish and English relations as a child because of her mixed parentage, her father being Scottish-Jewish, from Edinburgh, and her mother being English, of mixed Jewish and non-Jewish background, from Watford – her family would spend the annual summer holidays with Spark's grandparents in Watford until, when she was eight years old, her grandfather died and her grandmother moved to live with the family in Edinburgh (*CV*, 21, 86). As a child she sensed a split between Scottish and English identities. She recounts feeling embarrassed when her (English) mother came to collect her at school, and describes how English people were considered 'superficial and hypocritical' and 'over-dressed', and how her mother in fact dressed differently from other mothers, and spoke differently, in terms of accent and idiom – this was in contrast to her father, whose speech and dress were standard for the Edinburgh of the time, and thus no cause of embarrassment to the young Muriel, who sensed that the English were less tolerated than 'foreigners' (*CV*, 21–2). She also notes that her mother would talk of 'taps', which her father would call 'wells', and remembers a rough children's game involving the opponents representing the Scottish and the English – the Scottish and the Irish was another version (*CV*, 22). Of course the fact of the English being unpopular but not considered foreign suggests a complex relationship between the terms Scottish, English and the unmentioned term, British, which she does not expand on explicitly. She does however mention a puritanical atmosphere that she recalls in Edinburgh at this time (*CV*, 57, 79), although this did not lead to an emphasis on differences in doctrines between religions at her school, which was officially Presbyterian (*CV*, 53). The Calvinist background in Edinburgh in fact was an important theme in her early novel, *The Prime of Miss Jean Brodie*.[6] The account of growing up in Edinburgh is also rich in details of everyday life in the city, descriptions of the tenements and the shops she was familiar with, giving a strong sense of the city's formative influence on her.[7]

In a section of the third chapter (*CV*, 81–7) she describes her Watford grandparents and their background in detail. They kept a small shop. Her grandfather, Tom Uezzell, was the son of Watford corn-merchants, and his family name was a rare English name, originally derived from French (*CV*, 82). Her grandmother, Adelaide, had, according to Spark, a Jewish father and a Christian mother (*CV*, 85). This is an important assertion, since, according to the traditional Jewish matrilineal principle, Adelaide would not therefore automatically have been Jewish according to Jewish law (without converting), nor would Spark's mother, or Spark herself. The question of whether Adelaide was Jewish or not was the cause of controversy, both when it came to her burial, as Spark recounts, and later in Spark's difficult relations with her son, who believed that Adelaide had been Jewish, and therefore so had the whole family down to himself.[8] The issue of the matrilineal line also plays a role in *The Mandelbaum Gate*, in which Spark makes the protagonist, who broadly represents Spark herself, Jewish on her mother's side and English on the father's, the reverse of what she understood her own situation to be. There were also two great-aunts in Watford, Nancy and Sally, sisters of Tom, who were devoted Anglicans, and fond of mentioning the vicar in conversation when the young Muriel visited (*CV*, 84). These aunts contributed to the controversy over whether Adelaide was Jewish or Christian by putting a notice in the *Watford Observer* when Adelaide died that 'she fell asleep in Jesus' (*CV*, 84–5). Spark recounts that Adelaide had belonged to various church groups (of various churches) in Watford, but believes that she treated them as social opportunities (she was also a suffragette and had taken an interest in Spiritualism). The Watford

---

6   See, for example, Alan Bold, *Muriel Spark* (London: Methuen, 1986), 65.
7   In her essay 'Edinburgh-born', *Critical Essays on Muriel Spark*, Joseph Hynes, ed. (New York: G. K. Hall, 1992), 21, she states that she sees herself as an exile from Edinburgh.
8   For the controversy between Spark and her son see Stannard, *Muriel Spark*, 518.

Women's Church Union sent a gravestone to Edinburgh, which did not remain in place long because the cemetery was Jewish (*CV*, 84–5). These details are given drily and without extensive comment in *Curriculum Vitae*; they form the basis for her short story 'The Gentile Jewesses', as well as contributing, in modified forms, to the picture drawn of Barbara's background in *The Mandelbaum Gate*. Spark's two Jewish married aunts in Edinburgh, Rae and Esther, are also briefly mentioned (and her father's younger sister, Gertie, lived at their home for a period). The elder of the two, Esther, was practising (but not 'absolutely orthodox'), so that Spark's mother had to hide non-kosher foods in the house when she came to visit (*CV*, 45). So a picture of divisions in her background between her Scottish and English, Jewish and Gentile sides, emerges in her autobiography, but not a sense of strong tension between the elements, or any account of how they might come to be reconciled. Her brief mention of her conversion towards the end of the book does not present it as a repudiation of any previous part of her identity or background – rather, Catholicism 'corresponded to what I had always felt and known and believed' (*CV*, 202). 'The Gentile Jewesses' adds deeper reflections on her understanding of her complex background to the rather bare facts recounted in *Curriculum Vitae*.

The Prime of Miss Jean Brodie

Muriel Spark's novel, *The Prime of Miss Jean Brodie*, first published in 1961, does not directly address the theme of a character negotiating conflicts in his or her religious and national identity, but it does give insight into how Spark saw the influence of Calvinism as having shaped the culture of her native city, Edinburgh, amplifying the brief indications in *Curriculum Vitae*. Given that her description of this Calvinistically flavoured Edinburgh atmosphere has a critical edge, it is possible that there may have been an element of rebellion against this in her (later) conversion to Catholicism, just as Sandy the protagonist's becoming a Catholic nun at the end of the novel appears as a rebellion against, or rejection of, the non-Catholic milieu in which she grew up, especially at school. An indication that Sandy has reacted against the influences of her childhood comes when she is visited by someone who has also grown up in Edinburgh, after she has entered the convent, who points out that the influences of one's youth are important, to which she assents, with the qualification 'even if they provide something to react against' (*PMJB*, 35). Sandy, at this point, though, identifies 'a Miss Brodie in her prime' (*PMJB*, 35) as her main influence, rather than Calvinism, as proposed by her visitor.

The novel is narrated from the point of view of Sandy Stranger, a pupil at a girls' school in Edinburgh. She is in the class of the charismatic teacher, Miss Jean Brodie, who particularly cultivates a small set of girls, to which Sandy belongs, referred to by Miss Brodie as the 'crème de la crème' (*PMJB*, 8, for example), and she continues to mentor them after they are no longer in her class.[9] Miss Brodie is loosely based on a teacher who taught Spark as a young girl at her Edinburgh school.[10] Jean Brodie is interested in various subjects, often with Italian connections, such as Italian painting, and the fascist movement then in the ascendant in Italy, and she tries to share her interests with her set. She eventually loses her job at the school when Sandy, though a member of her set, betrays her, by revealing to the headmistress what Miss Brodie's political sympathies are. The novel is full of details connecting the atmosphere of Edinburgh with its Calvinist heritage, as well as comments on national identity reminiscent of Spark's memories as recorded in *Curriculum Vitae*.

Spark gives Sandy an English mother, whose linguistic differences from Edinburgh people (calling her daughter 'darling' instead of 'dear') and differences in dress (dressing more luxuriously) lead to embarrassment

---

9 Miss Brodie has 'predestined' her set – the connection between the Brodie set and the doctrine of predestination is pointed out, for example, by Bold, *Muriel Spark*, 65, and a similar point is made by Bryan Cheyette, *Muriel Spark* (Tavistock: Northcote House, 2000), 55.

10 Spark writes about Miss Christina Kay, the inspiration for Miss Jean Brodie, and discusses how Miss Brodie and Miss Kay are related, in her autobiography *Curriculum Vitae*, 56–70.

for Sandy (*PMJB*, 18) – this experience is similar to Spark's embarrassment at her own mother's Englishness, and a factor in Sandy's being a 'stranger', as her name suggests.[11] The religious affiliations of Miss Brodie and the members of the set are listed early in the novel (*PMJB*, 35–6), and Sandy and two others are presented as belonging to 'believing though not church-going families'; so Sandy's background of religious practice is similar to Spark's own, as described in her autobiography. Miss Brodie on the other hand adheres to 'strict Church of Scotland habits' (*PMJB*, 36) such as keeping the Sabbath, but also attends evening classes at Edinburgh University in comparative religion, which she tells her class about, and recommends the Gospels to her pupils in a positive but vague way ('But the girls were set to the Gospels with diligence for their truth and goodness, and to read them aloud with their beauty'. *PMJB*, 36) So it is not doctrinal Calvinism that Miss Brodie represents, but she carries Calvinistic habits, while being vague about doctrine – a position comparable to how Spark describes her school's religious stance. The lack of insistence on doctrinal details allowed Spark's school a tolerant attitude to other religions, as Spark remembers in *Curriculum Vitae*, but in Miss Brodie's case this vagueness can be seen as opening the way for her philosophical Romanticism, which in turn leads her in the direction of an attachment to fascist politics. Sandy's later becoming a Catholic nun is thus a reaction against Miss Brodie's non-doctrinal religion, as well as her cultural Calvinism (Miss Brodie even suspects Sandy of having become a nun just to annoy her, *PMJB*, 63). Jean Brodie attends churches belonging to a variety of denominations on Sundays by rota, but all of Protestant denominations, or 'any other church outside the Roman Catholic pale which she might discover' (*PMJB*, 85). This is because she believes that the Catholic Church is 'a church of superstition, and that only people who did not want to think for themselves were Roman Catholics' (*PMJB*, 85). Miss Brodie in fact makes this same comment again later, when questioning Sandy as to why she would want to have an affair with Teddy Lloyd, the Catholic art teacher, who as a Catholic 'can't think for himself'

---

[11] The significance of Sandy's surname is noted, for example, by Cheyette, *Muriel Spark*, 56.

(*PMJB*, 123). Spark's frustration at prejudices against Catholics held by non-Catholics is also expressed in *The Mandelbaum Gate* when the English wife of a diplomat gives voice to such views in the presence of the protagonist, Barbara. In the same paragraph in which Miss Brodie's habit of attending various non-Catholic churches has been noted the narrator goes on to make the interesting suggestion that Miss Brodie 'was by temperament suited only to the Roman Catholic Church' and that 'possibly it [the Catholic Church] could have embraced, even while it disciplined, her soaring and diving spirit, it might even have normalized her' (*PMJB*, 85). The narrator then speculates that 'perhaps this was the reason that she shunned it, lover of Italy though she was, bringing to her support a rigid Edinburgh-born side of herself when the Catholic Church was in question, although this side was not otherwise greatly in evidence' (*PMJB*, 85). Spark seems to be arguing here that the Catholic Church could have given Miss Brodie the firm framework she needed, from a moral, spiritual and intellectual point of view, to allow her to flourish, discouraging her from moving in some of the directions which proved to be destructive for her. She tells us that Miss Brodie has some awareness that the Catholic Church could discipline her, but wishes to protect her freedom, and protects it, ironically, by invoking her culturally Calvinist background, with its traditional anti-Catholic orientation, although she does not let this background limit her in other ways. Spark's point here is anti-Romantic, in that she does not endorse Miss Brodie's quest for pure freedom when it is the freedom to destroy oneself.

In the same paragraph which details the religious affiliations of the girls of the Brodie set, and in the preceding paragraph, Sandy's reactions to Edinburgh churches are compared to her reaction to a picture of Cologne Cathedral shown to the class by Miss Brodie. Sandy is scared of old Edinburgh churches on the outside, and does not want to go into St Giles Cathedral on a trip through Edinburgh's Old Town with the Brodie set – these churches are of dark stone and 'were built so warningly with their upraised fingers' (*PMJB*, 35). However she finds Scottish churches 'more reassuring' (*PMJB*, 35) inside (than Cologne Cathedral), because they contain only people and no ghosts during services – later on in the paragraph it is explained that she believes in ghosts. By contrast, Cologne Cathedral (a Catholic church, though this is not specified) in the picture is 'like a wedding cake, which looked as if it had been built for pleasure and festivities, and parties given by the Prodigal Son in his early career' (*PMJB*, 35). However, since it is stated that the inside of Scottish churches is 'more reassuring' – by implication more reassuring than Cologne Cathedral, which was being talked about in the previous sentence – it seems that Sandy imagines that there would be ghosts inside Cologne Cathedral during a service, although this is not made explicit. Spark is known for her insistence, in her novels, on the reality of both the material and the spiritual world, and here she may be expressing, through Sandy, an intuition of her own to the effect that despite the seriousness of aspect characteristic of Edinburgh's Protestant churches, they do not contain spiritual presences other than live people. So Sandy's belief in ghosts stands for a belief in the reality of the spiritual world, and the possibility of its presence in the everyday material world. It was part of the attraction of Catholicism to Spark, as well as to Waugh, that they saw it as espousing this view of reality, in contrast to the national churches of Britain.[12]

Spark also uses religious and national identity to portray the tension between Miss Brodie and other more conventional colleagues, who resent her experimental methods, and to show how this tension is subtly manifested. There had been no overt hostility, but Miss Brodie's colleagues in the Junior School had been in the habit of saying 'good morning' to her 'with predestination in their smiles' (*PMJB*, 75). Spark's decision to describe Miss Brodie's colleagues' withering smiles with reference to the Calvinist doctrine of predestination, since Scotland's majority church, the Church of Scotland, was founded on Calvinist teachings, suggests that, as Spark sees it, being the outsider in the Edinburgh society of her childhood meant being outside the culturally Calvinist consensus – even if Miss Brodie was in some ways a product of it. Another way the tension between Miss Brodie and her colleagues is manifested, is in the way 'good morning' is said. The

---

12 The work Sandy is writing as a nun is entitled 'The Transfiguration of the Commonplace', and this theme can also be read as representing Spark's conviction that the spiritual coexists with the material and interacts with it – Karl Malkoff, *Muriel Spark* (New York: Columbia University Press, 1968), 3, sees the title as a description of Spark's fictional method.

tone of the way Miss Brodie's colleagues say it, 'in a more than Edinburgh manner' (*PMJB*, 54), gives Sandy the feeling that they are really saying 'I scorn you' (*PMJB*, 54), whereas Miss Brodie replies with an English pronunciation – her response, sounding to the Scottish ear like 'Good mawning' (*PMJB*, 54), is 'more than ever anglicised in its accent than was its usual proud wont' (*PMJB*, 54). Here tending towards an English pronunciation is a sign of being an outsider, and even of rebellion.

An irony in the novel is that Sandy, who later becomes a nun, makes her first contact with Catholicism through her affair with Teddy Lloyd, the Anglo-Welsh art teacher, who is a Catholic (so an outsider in several ways), and who has numerous children, a fact attributed by Miss Brodie to his and his wife's being Catholics (*PMJB*, 92) – elsewhere the narrator comments that 'The Lloyds were Catholics and so were made to have a lot of children by force' (*PMJB*, 102), a statement which parodies popular (in Sandy's environment) views of Catholics. An important theme of Spark's, which emerges clearly in *The Mandelbaum Gate*, is that the entire history of a person can contribute to his or her achievement of spiritual development, and that episodes that in themselves consist in actions which are not praiseworthy, can nevertheless unexpectedly lead to opportunities for spiritual growth. Just as Barbara's affair with Harry Clegg is the beginning of her recognition that she has been leading a self-centred life, opening up the opportunity for her to become less egotistical, Sandy's affair with Teddy Lloyd, apparently accidentally, makes her aware of a religious tradition within which there is the opportunity for her later to pursue a monastic vocation.

In the most extended passage on Calvinism, late in the novel, in the fifth chapter, the narrator describes how Sandy, who is now old enough to walk around Edinburgh by herself, and already becoming close to Teddy Lloyd, 'would go and stand outside St Giles Cathedral or the Tolbooth, and contemplate these emblems of a dark and terrible salvation which made the fires of the damned seem very merry to the imagination by contrast, and much preferable' (*PMJB*, 108). The narrator goes on to complain, on Sandy's behalf, that she has grown up without anything very clear to rebel against, because in her middle-class social milieu she has not heard Calvinism talked of 'except as a joke that had once been taken seriously' (*PMJB*, 108), whereas in social groups above or below her own she would have gathered experience of real Calvinism, if she had been aware of such groups. In her own social environment, in her suburb and school, her experiences had been, at least superficially, similar to those she might have had in any equivalent place in the British Isles, for example, 'in Ealing' (*PMJB*, 108). She had however realized that 'some quality of life peculiar to Edinburgh and nowhere else had been going on unbeknown to her all the time' and 'however undesirable it might be ... she desired to know what it was, and to cease to be protected from it by enlightened people' (*PMJB*, 108). The narrator specifies that it is 'the religion of Calvin' of which she feels deprived, 'or rather a specified recognition of it', because it was her 'birthright', 'something definite to reject' (*PMJB*, 108). While, the narrator goes on to explain, she later discovered that the doctrine of predestination according to Calvin was as disturbing as the popular imagination of it, she had nevertheless found the genuinely Calvinist teachers at her school, who admitted to believing in predestination, 'In some ways the most real and rooted people' she knew (*PMJB*, 108). Spark here seems to be indicating that while Sandy rejects both the relativism of her immediate social environment and the overt Calvinism of other social groups in Edinburgh, a move presumably approved of by Spark as it is the move she made herself, nevertheless straightforward Calvinism is to be preferred to relativism, because it offers definite proposals which can be accepted or rejected, rather than failing to offer any choice, but rather, perhaps, co-opting the young person by claiming to encompass any moral or religious position, as relativism does. Spark has already, earlier in the novel, made it clear that it is not a religion's or moral code's imposition of limits that she objects to, when she suggests that Miss Brodie's failure to recognize any limits on herself is destructive for her – so it is rather Calvinism's putting of limits in the wrong places, than its putting of limits at all, that Spark presents as deserving to be reacted against.

The mode in which Sandy knows what the previous paragraph has explained, is next outlined: 'Sandy was unable to formulate these exciting propositions; nevertheless she experienced them in the air she breathed, she sensed them in the curiously defiant way in which the people she knew broke the Sabbath, and she smelt them in the excesses of Miss Brodie in her prime' (*PMJB*, 109). What Spark is describing here is the kind of implicit knowledge described by Newman, for example, in his sermon 'The Theory of Developments in Religious Doctrine',[13] but also in many other places, which apprehends a situation as an idea, but is unable to articulate what it has apprehended (though the articulation may come later). Sandy senses the effects of Calvinism in the society she lives in, though she cannot yet articulate what she has detected, and part of what she senses is the way that Calvinism influences even those parts of society which do not profess it. So, for example, breaking Calvinist rules is done with the consciousness of the rules one is breaking, and Sandy also sees a rebellion against Calvinism in Miss Brodie's extravagant Romanticism. What Sandy had understood about Miss Brodie's rebellion is then made clearer in the following sentence: 'In this oblique way she began to sense what went to the makings of Miss Brodie who had elected herself to grace in so particular a way and with more exotic suicidal enchantment than if she had simply taken to drink like other spinsters who couldn't stand it any more' (*PMJB*, 109). So Miss Brodie, while rebelling against her Calvinist background and the Calvinist culture of Edinburgh, has staged a rebellion with a Calvinist shape, as Spark explains it, and Sandy senses it, one which involved a distorted or transposed version of the doctrine of predestination, one in which she can elect herself (the idea that Miss Brodie behaves as if she was God is one of the themes of the novel). That Jean Brodie sees herself in this way constitutes one of the principal criticisms of her expressed by the narrator, and in the last chapter Sandy criticizes her in thought, because Miss Brodie 'thinks she is Providence ... she thinks she is the God of Calvin, she sees the beginning and the end', a conclusion Sandy is led to in reaction against her teacher's planning for one of her set, Rose, to become Teddy Lloyd's lover in Miss Brodie's place.[14] Sandy will rebel not just against the straightforward Calvinism of many of Edinburgh's residents, but also against Calvinist-shaped rebellions against Calvinism, such as Miss Brodie's. The teacher has rejected Calvinism's strict rules, but retained its concept of the elect, albeit

---

13 John Henry Newman, *Fifteen Sermons Preached Before the University of Oxford Between A.D. 1826 and 1843* (Notre Dame, IN: University of Notre Dame Press, 1997), 312–51.
14 Peter Kemp, *Muriel Spark* (London: Paul Elek, 1974), 80, notes that Miss Brodie tries to treat the girls of her set as 'creations subject to her purposes'.

qualified by the notion that she can nominate herself as a member of the elect, and this combination, Spark suggests in the novel, is consonant with a form of Romanticism, a solipsistic form which tempts the adherent to manipulate others for the adherent's own benefit or amusement.

The narrator, late in the novel, describes how through her affair Sandy becomes interested in Teddy Lloyd's mind, one of the elements of which is his Catholicism (she is initially interested in his mind because she realizes that he is in love with Jean Brodie, and is fascinated by this fact), and she later loses her interest in him, but retains it in his religion – her mind was full of it 'as a night sky is full of things visible and invisible' (*PMJB*, 123), a description which, again, is reminiscent of Newman's theory of how an idea can be held partly or wholly implicitly, rather than explicitly. In this case the simile seems to suggest that she holds the Catholic idea in a partly explicit, partly implicit way. The simile may also remind the reader of Spark's basic conviction that the world is composed of material and spiritual elements, both of which are real.

Spark balances her presentation of Sandy's conversion to Catholicism from Calvinism by mentioning that she met 'quite a number of fascists much less agreeable than Miss Brodie' in the Catholic Church. This is not a sign, though, that Sandy has made a mistake in her move, one which Spark made herself (though Spark did not become a nun).[15] The novel arguably does not present Sandy as a more attractive character than Miss Brodie, and cultivates an ambiguity as to whether Sandy's 'betrayal' of Miss Brodie really is a betrayal, or an act of responsibility.[16] The novel nevertheless clearly presents Miss Brodie's position as intellectually flawed, criticizes her actions for being manipulative and even argues that Miss Brodie herself could have benefited from becoming a Catholic.

Although the matter of national and religious identity is not the principal theme in *The Prime of Miss Jean Brodie*, it constitutes an important

---

15 Spark herself disliked many individual Catholics whom she met, as mentioned, for example, by Malkoff, *Muriel Spark*, 5. See also Cheyette, *Muriel Spark*, 57, who sees Sandy's move as being from the determinism of Calvinism to the free will of Catholicism.

16 Malkoff, *Muriel Spark*, 32, notes that Miss Brodie and Sandy are in fact similar, and discusses how she obtains insight into herself and reality by means of Miss Brodie.

secondary strand. As our discussion has shown, many of the points made about religious and national identity in *Curriculum Vitae* are echoed in *The Prime of Miss Jean Brodie* (and they will be taken up again in 'The Gentile Jewesses' and *The Mandelbaum Gate*). As Spark's novels are often partially autobiographical, and much of what happens in *The Prime of Miss Jean Brodie* is described as deriving from Spark's childhood experience in *Curriculum Vitae*, and she talks there of the correspondences between the novel and her own life, the novel can be looked to for clues about her own attitudes to Edinburgh and her experiences of growing up. Spark's own conversion to Catholicism occurred long after she had moved away from Edinburgh, when she was living in London, and after her time in southern Africa, but given that she describes her conversion, in *Curriculum Vitae*, as being the fruit of a long process (*CV*, 202), it is not unrealistic to see something of Sandy's rebellion against the culturally Calvinist atmosphere of her school years in Spark's own spiritual journey. The attitude that Spark gives to Sandy with respect to the Calvinism of Edinburgh is complex, in that it shows a certain respect for strict Calvinism, while seeming to find the tolerant post-Calvinism of her middle-class surroundings particularly intellectually flawed, though well-meaning. Spark, a very unsentimental writer, has Sandy react in the way that she would react herself to anything that appeared to her incoherent, that is, by rejecting it, but Sandy's reaction is to reject both strict Calvinism and post-Calvinist secularism, which the novel shows as functioning as reactions against each other in Edinburgh society – instead she adopts that position which both strict Calvinism and post-Calvinism would agree in opposing, that is, Catholicism. Thus Spark in this novel portrays Catholicism as 'the other' in the context of Edinburgh society. Sandy has always been the other, because of her English connections, as Spark was because of her English and Jewish connections – however Sandy is not shown cutting her connections with Edinburgh after her conversion and her becoming a nun (although the novel does not describe her post-conversion life in any detail), whereas Spark had already left Scotland behind permanently by the time of her conversion, so neither Spark's life nor the novel addresses the issue of how the otherness of living in Edinburgh as a Catholic could be overcome.

'The Gentile Jewesses'

'The Gentile Jewesses' is a very short short story (about eight pages long), first published in 1963, two years before *The Mandelbaum Gate*, and can be seen as a rehearsal of some of the issues which feature in the novel. The story is based on a description of Spark's maternal grandparents, and she refers to it as 'nearly factual' in *Curriculum Vitae* (*CV*, 81), but the narrative expands on the information given there. As the title of the story suggests, the main theme is Spark's grandmother's split identity, with some reference to Spark's mother and Spark herself sharing in this split identity. In the story the grandmother (Adelaide, but usually referred to as 'my grandmother' in the story) has a Jewish father and a Gentile mother, as in *Curriculum Vitae*, and the extra information is provided that she is from Stepney (GJ, 348) – an area of East London with Jewish associations. Spark recounts that she asks the grandmother, after the grandmother has moved from Watford to the family home in Edinburgh, whether she is Jewish or Gentile, and she replies, 'I am a Gentile Jewess' (GJ, 349). There follows a description of the grandmother's ambiguous religious identity. When still living in England, she belongs to the Mother's Union, which is affiliated to the Church of England, and attends Methodist, Baptist and Quaker social events, but does not attend church on Sundays, and speaks of God as 'the Almighty' (GJ, 350–1). She does not recognize any kinship between herself and a family of Polish Jewish immigrants who move into her area in Watford, viewing them as 'foreigners', but, on the other hand, tells the young Muriel about how 'her ancestors on her father's side' crossed the Red Sea (GJ, 351). Muriel's mother's religious and spiritual practices are related, at the end of the story, and they too are ambiguous. She bows three times to the new moon, and lights Sabbath candles on Friday nights, saying a prayer in inaccurate Hebrew; she keeps a picture of Jesus wearing the crown of thorns in a locket in her handbag, as well as statues of Buddha and the Venus de Milo at home (GJ, 345). Both Spark's parents are described as being non-specific in their religious beliefs, but they believe in 'the Almighty' (GJ, 345).[17]

The story also stresses that there is a non-Jewish, Anglican English side to Spark's background. The grandfather, Tom, is presented as blond and freckled (GJ, 348, 350), and his devout Anglican unmarried sisters, Sally and Nancy, who live together and are visited by the young Muriel every summer, make their appearance, as they do in *Curriculum Vitae*. Tom was dispossessed by his family for marrying Adelaide (GJ, 348), but was later 'frigidly' reconciled with his sisters (GJ, 352). It is not altogether clear what the family's objection was: in the same sentence that the dispossession is mentioned the information that Adelaide was fifteen years older than Tom is included, as if this may be the reason for Tom's family's objection, rather than her being partly Jewish. However a subject of conversation on Muriel's visits is the fact that she, unlike her grandmother, does not look Jewish, though Muriel is a 'Gentile Jewess' because her father is Jewish (GJ, 352). The young Muriel takes advantage of their credulity and lack of knowledge about Jewish people by making up spurious facts, which they believe, such as that her small feet are a Jewish characteristic (which she invents in order to convince them that she does after all look Jewish), and that Jewish people are all engineers, like her father (GJ, 352).

The story concludes that when Spark became a Catholic, to her parents 'it was no great shock … since with Roman Catholics too, it all boils down to the Almighty in the end' (GJ, 354). As a whole, the story presents Spark's mixed background in a way which shows that her pondering on this topic was in part the stimulus for writing *The Mandelbaum Gate*, and her method of slightly adjusting details in order to create a fictional character, closely based on, but distinguishable from, herself is clear to see when novel and story are compared. In *The Mandelbaum Gate* the conflict

17   Gerard Carruthers, 'Muriel Spark as Catholic Novelist', *The Edinburgh Companion to Muriel Spark*, Michael Gardiner and Willy Maley, eds (Cambridge: Cambridge University Press, 2010), 76, argues that Spark states her parents' religious convictions using banal language in order to link the sacred and the profane. He also (77) suggests that, through the complications in the maternal line, her Jewish identity is asserted and denied at the same time.

between the Jewish and non-Jewish elements in the protagonist, Barbara, is heightened in comparison to the biographical situation by giving Barbara orthodox Jewish relatives, and making her closest non-Jewish relative, her grandmother, a church-going Anglican, whereas in Spark's own family the Jewish-Christian divide did not seem important to them, except for the maiden aunts. Thus the implied conviction in the biographical situation is that on Spark's part, there no sense that she is rejecting anything in her background by becoming a Catholic; her reading of Newman is likely to have contributed to this position, together with the easygoing and doctrinally vague approach of her parents and maternal grandparents. In *The Mandelbaum Gate* the sense of a division to be overcome is made much clearer than it appears to have been in Spark's own personal life.

The Mandelbaum Gate

First published in 1965, *The Mandelbaum Gate* is an unusual novel in Spark's oeuvre: it is long (slightly over 300 pages in the Penguin edition) compared with her usually very concise works, and it is introspective in a way not typical for her.[18] It is set in the Holy Land in 1961, and follows the extended visit and pilgrimage of the protagonist, Barbara Vaughan – Spark herself made a similar trip in the same year, although she adds completely fictional elements to Barbara's journey, such as a romance between Barbara and an archaeologist, which began before the start of the journey and eventually leads to their marrying, and to an adventure involving espionage in which Barbara is accidentally caught up. Barbara is a Catholic convert, with a mixed London Jewish and rural English background, and her trip to the Holy Land, as well as being a religious pilgrimage, is presented as a personal quest, a chance to reflect on various divisions in her character and

---

18   Bold, *Muriel Spark*, 78, notes that Spark later had misgivings about the novel due to its greater emotional content compared with her others.

background. Besides her Jewish-Gentile division, she is portrayed as being divided between the passionate and intellectual sides to her personality, and she is in the midst of a crisis regarding whether she should marry the object of her romantic attachment, Harry Clegg, who is working near the Dead Sea on an excavation at the same time that she is visiting the Holy Land. She fears she may not be able to marry him in the Church, because he is a divorcee, and she is considering whether she should rather continue living with a single woman friend, Miss Rickworth (the headmistress of a school at which Barbara also teaches), as she has been doing before the journey. At the time when the novel is set, the Holy Land, and Jerusalem itself – Jerusalem being the focus for much of the novel (and the location of the Mandelbaum Gate of the title) – is divided between Israel and Jordan, and Spark uses this division as an emblem of Barbara's own divisions.[19]

Barbara exhibits a split identity characterized by many elements of Spark's own, but it is simplified, and the contrasts sharpened. An important simplification Spark makes is to eliminate the Scottish-English axis of contrast in her own background, and to make both Barbara's sides, her mother's and father's, English – English Jewish (possibly with Central European origins, as indicated by the faulty English of one of the elder relatives, *MG*, 37) and English Anglican. Barbara's mother is English Jewish, and her father was English Anglican. There is also no indication of complexity in the mother's or father's background – unlike in Spark's own case, who was more than half Jewish, whereas Barbara is split into tidy opposing halves. Barbara's father, a rural English Anglican from Worcestershire, died in a riding accident during her childhood. Her mother remarries and moves to Paris, sending the young Barbara to a boarding school, and she has, while growing up, divided her time during the holidays between her father's family, the Vaughans, in Worcestershire, and her mother's family, the Aaronsons, who live in London's Golders Green. So there is a clear

---

19 Irving Malin, 'The Deceptions of Muriel Spark', *The Vision Obscured: Perceptions of Some Twentieth-Century Catholic Novelists*, Melvin J. Friedman, ed. (New York: Fordham University Press, 1970), 107, sees the Gate as representing unity underlying the division, since it is named after a single house on the street which it then divided.

urban-rural divide parallel to the Jewish-Anglican divide, and, in what might seem something of a stereotype, the Jewish family is intellectual and the rural Anglican family is sporting. In all these aspects Spark makes the division starker than it was in her own background. In her case her Watford family was not altogether rural, although Watford appears as a small town surrounded by countryside in *Curriculum Vitae*. Barbara, growing up, wants to belong to both sides of her family, and wants each side fully to accept that she belongs to the other side as well, but she finds this difficult to achieve. She recalls, in one of the many flashbacks with which the novel's action is interspersed, that she was not allowed to help with washing up and related tasks in the Golders Green kitchen, because she did not know the kosher rules, and she admits that she lacked a will to learn them (*MG*, 35–7). On the other hand, as part of the same set of recollections, she remembers her English grandmother trying to persuade her that there is no need for her to leave in a hurry in order to arrive at her London family's house in time for Passover – she assures Barbara that she does not look Jewish at all (*MG*, 31–2). There is perhaps an echo of the Spark Anglican aunts' similar views on the young Muriel's appearance, as recorded in *Curriculum Vitae*.

Her grandmother's attempt to dissuade her from precipitate departure to London for Passover comes as part of a group of recollections which juxtaposes the two sets of religious influences Barbara was exposed to as a child. The week before, she has celebrated Anglican Easter with her Anglican family, and she arrives just in time for the Passover festival, the ritual of which is described in detail. This is a ceremony at which Barbara, when younger, had played the role of the youngest person present, asking the eldest in Hebrew the ceremonial question as to the reason for the celebration, although on the occasion described a German refugee plays this role (*MG*, 33–5). This description has been understood by Judy Sproxton[20] as an anticipation of Barbara's later participation in the Catholic Eucharist – in fact both the Passover ceremony and the Anglican celebration, occurring in quick succession, can be seen as containing elements which are to be

---

20 Judy Sproxton, *The Women of Muriel Spark* (London: Constable, 1992), 33.

found in the Catholic Mass. It is also mentioned, during the recollections of the Passover ceremony, that Barbara's older relatives had been hoping she would find a Jewish husband, not believing 'that her Gentile relatives could be particularly well disposed to her' (*MG*, 34), thus reinforcing the point that both sets of relatives had been 'innocently obtuse about her true identity' (*MG*, 31), that is, her mixed identity.

Barbara recalls that the younger members of the family, though they viewed themselves as agnostics, nevertheless felt their Jewishness during the Passover ceremonies, and that she also, who had agreed with them to espouse agnosticism during the previous Christmas holidays, is included in the ceremonies, 'because, after all, blood was blood, and you inherit from your mother's side' (*MG*, 34). One of the important changes that Spark has made between her own and Barbara's backgrounds is highlighted here. Spark herself was Jewish on her father's side, and mixed on her mother's side, with no continuous Jewish maternal line from her mother, according to her presentation of her background in *Curriculum Vitae*, and she made no changes to this in 'The Gentile Jewesses'.[21] She was thus not, she believed, automatically Jewish according to the matrilineal principle, so her reversing the position for Barbara is interesting, even if the reason for it is not clear. It seems possible that by making it open for Barbara to consider herself Jewish without going through a difficult conversion process, as she might have had to do if her Jewish side had been her father's side, Spark is emphasizing that her decision to become a Catholic has been a free decision, taken against the background that either the Anglican or Jewish paths would have been open to her.

In the novel these reflections are initially provoked by a conversation between Barbara and a Polish-Israeli travel guide, as well as conversations with her Israeli friend Saul Ephraim. The exchange with the Polish-Israeli guide takes place while he is driving her to the north of Israel on a tour, and she recalls it while driving herself to Mount Tabor, the site of her recollections on her childhood holidays: this is in the second chapter,

---

21 Cheyette, *Muriel Spark*, 75–6, notes this switch in which parent is Jewish between Spark and Barbara.

'Barbara Vaughan's Identity'. The guide questions what she means by saying that she is half-Jewish, and asks on which side she is Jewish – on learning that it is her mother's side, he insists, 'You are then a full Jew by the Law' (*MG*, 27). Barbara rejects this conclusion, on the basis that she would not be fully Jewish according to the non-Jewish parent's law, and also reveals that she was not brought up in any religion. She rejects the guide's suggestion, however, that by becoming a Catholic she is denying her Jewishness: 'I don't deny it. I've just been telling you about it' (*MG*, 27). Her initial reaction to the questions is to feel 'displaced' (*MG*, 27), as if she is losing her identity under the analysis, but later in the day she attempts to explain her background to the guide, starting with the biblical phrase 'I am who I am' (*MG*, 28), but then going into detail and leaving the guide 'bewildered' (*MG*, 28). She does not feel however as if she has succeeded in answering his repeated question about why she had become a Catholic, given that, religiously, she was already Jewish through her mother. Having failed to explain her conversion to her guide, she tries with Saul Ephraim, who that evening suggests to her that it is not surprising that Israeli guides find it difficult to understand her identity, given that she is British, a Catholic convert and half-Jewish: 'The three together are a lot' (*MG*, 31).

In another conversation with Saul Ephraim, which takes place while they are visiting Jaffa together, she tries to explain how her Catholicism is not, to her, incompatible with her also having a Jewish identity. She has been telling him how she tried to remind both sets of her relatives, during her childhood, of her other set. She expands on her feelings about her split identity, however, saying that it is not only a matter of the two halves, but that there is something beyond: 'There's the human soul, the individual ... Something unique and unrepeatable' (*MG*, 37). She is perhaps expressing her more mature reflections, rather than those she had as a child, and giving a suggestion of the idea that a move away from an inward-looking analysis of the self, the kind of analysis which made her feel that she was losing her identity under questioning from the Polish-Israeli tour guide, is necessary to find a sense of wholeness. Saul Ephraim, however, makes the same kind of challenge as the tour guide did, asking her why she chose 'the Gentile side' in the end, insisting that becoming a Catholic constituted choosing that side (*MG*, 37). Barbara is equally insistent that she did not make that kind of choice – 'I didn't choose any side at any time' (*MG*, 37) – and further makes a number of important statements on how she views the relationship between Judaism and Catholicism. She denies that Catholicism is a Gentile religion, saying that '… it started off as a new ordering of the Jewish religion' (*MG*, 38), and, to the objection that it has changed since then, she insists, 'It's still a new order of an older firm' (*MG*, 38).[22] She understands Catholicism as including her Jewish heritage, not as a rejection of it.

Also in Jaffa, apparently earlier on during the day, possibly just before the above conversation, and separated from it in the chapter by episodes with her guides recalled while on Mount Tabor and reminiscences of childhood, Barbara remarks to Saul, 'that the Scriptures were specially important to the half-Jew turned Catholic. The Old Testament and the New, she said, were to her – as near as she could apply to her own experience the phrase of Dante's vision – "bound by love into one volume"' (*MG*, 26). The importance to her of the Bible, and of its inclusion of the Jewish scriptures together with the New Testament scriptures,[23] is clearly part of the importance of the Holy Land pilgrimage to Barbara, since she is visiting the sites at which most of the major events in both Testaments were enacted, and many of the locations she visits, especially Jerusalem, the novel's focus, have overlapping significances involving both Testaments.[24]

22   An example of a quotation from Newman's writings (in this case from his preconversion writings) which would support Spark's contention here is the following: 'Revealed Religion, as such, is of the nature of a positive rule, implying, as it does, an addition, greater or less, to the religion of nature, and the disclosure of facts, which are thus disclosed, because not otherwise discoverable. Accordingly, the difference between the state of Jews and Christians is one simply of degree' (Newman, *Fifteen Sermons*, 171). He is here arguing for the possibility of employing moral examples from the Old Testament to modern circumstances applying to Christians, on the basis that the Jewish religious system of the time is not incomparable with the Christian system of his time.
23   Silvana Caporaletti, *A World in a Grain of Sand: I romanzi di Muriel Spark* (Lecce: Milella, 2000), 286–7, stresses the idea of the two Testaments being united in Barbara.
24   Ruth Whittacker, *The Faith and Fiction of Muriel Spark* (London: Macmillan, 1982), 70, notes the way that Jerusalem unites the two Testaments, and thus Barbara goes there seeking to reunite her identity. According to Rodney Stenning Edgecombe, *Vocation and Identity in the Fiction of Muriel Spark* (Columbia: University of Missouri

Barbara's conversion to Catholicism has in fact given her a minority, outsider status in British society, just as having adopted Judaism would have done (as Poitou points out),[25] and the novel gives examples of the kind of anti-Catholic prejudice not uncommon among the non-Catholic portion of the British population at the time of the novel. One case is the wife of a British diplomat in Israel, Ruth Gardnor, whose dismissive comments on Catholicism to Barbara, made despite knowing that Barbara is a Catholic, are accompanied by Spark's comment on Barbara's behalf:

> This was nothing new to Barbara; ever since her conversion she had met sophisticated women who, on the subject of Catholicism, sneered like French village atheists, and expected to be excused from normal good manners, let alone intelligence, on this one subject. (*MG*, 265)

Barbara's friend, Miss Rickworth, the headmistress of a school at which Barbara works, displays the same prejudice:

> Barbara was already a Catholic when she had met Ricky [Miss Rickworth]; they had carefully avoided religious discussions; and only once or twice had she discerned Ricky's irritation with some observance of her religion, and felt irritation when Ricky let fall a remark about some Catholic dogma which revealed not only her disapproval, but also a muddled notion of what the dogma was. (*MG*, 161)

Barbara senses distaste and also ignorance in this British anti-Catholic prejudice, and it causes her to have a similar kind of difficulty in explaining herself as a Catholic in British society as she has had in explaining her mixed background in Israel. Specifically she has struggled to explain to British interlocutors why there may be a religious obstacle to her marrying Harry Clegg, due to his having been married before.

Barbara's divided personality is the dominant theme of the beginning of the novel, and while some of the splits and hesitations are not directly linked to her ethnic and religious background, Spark presents all the splits as culminating in the sense of crisis which precipitates the Holy

---

Press, 1990), 74, Barbara's childhood experiences with the two sides of her family can be compared to the two Testaments as seen by the Church Fathers.

25 Poitou, 'La rage d'être autre', 19.

Land journey. Her practical hesitations are as to whether to stay with Miss Rickworth, who expects her to remain,[26] or to leave her to marry Harry Clegg, and whether to marry Harry Clegg even if she cannot marry him in the Church: he is trying to obtain an annulment of his previous marriage, but the outcome is uncertain. However, one of the splits in her personality is correlated, in her understanding, with her divided background: she sees herself as divided in her personality into a restrained, intellectual side and a passionate side, and she has come to understand her restrained side as her English side and her passionate side as her Jewish side. Her restrained side is partly a matter of her education, due to her academic formation 'in the post-graduate tradition of a great university's English department' (*MG*, 22), and she has the thesis writer's tendency to select only relevant facts (*MG*, 23), leading to a feeling of limitation: 'All it meant was that her habits of mind were inadequate to cope with the whole of her experience, and thus Barbara Vaughan was in a state of conflict, like practically everyone else, in some mode or another' (*MG*, 23). Barbara's appearance matches this side of her personality. She has cultivated an outward look which leads Freddy Hamilton, a British diplomat and key character in the novel, to see her in the following way: 'His first impression had been of a pleasant English spinster …' (*MG*, 16).[27] She has, by appearing this way, led Miss Rickworth to believe that she has no intention of marrying, and therefore will never move out of their shared accommodation. The opposite to this 'English' side, her passionate side, she associates, without being sure why, with her Jewish side, a 'basic error with an elusive vapour of truth in it' (*MG*, 43) according to the narrating Spark, so that when she is staying with non-Jewish English cousins in St Albans before the journey to the Holy Land, to work on an archaeological site and pursue a secret affair with Harry Clegg, she

---

26 Anna Walczuk, *Irony as a Mode of Perception and Principle of Ordering Reality in the Novels of Muriel Spark* (Krakow: Universitas, 2008), 73–4, sees Barbara's journey to Jerusalem as partly motivated by a need to escape from the false identity imposed on her by Miss Rickworth.

27 Kemp, *Muriel Spark*, 100, notes that Spark in the novel criticizes the kind of classification in terms of social groups, ignoring individuals, which Freddy, for example, engages in.

sees her cousins, Miles and Kathy, a married couple, as lacking in passion, in marked contrast to herself, and views the difference in this regard between herself and them as being a result of their different ethnic make-up (*MG*, 43–4). Apart from the way Barbara aligns the fact of having a passionate nature with one rather than the other side of her ethnic background, we see her creating a narrative of herself as an outsider to English society, an outsider status which becoming Catholic has in fact reinforced.

Freddy Hamilton is the second most important character in the novel, and, as a fastidious, public-school-educated (and single) British diplomat, could be seen as representing the establishment British, or, more specifically, English, culture, to which Barbara is at least partially an outsider. The novel begins with Freddy, having spent a weekend with English friends on the Jordanian side of the boundary in Jerusalem, crossing back over the Mandelbaum Gate, and walking across the Ultra-Orthodox quarter, while pondering a rhymed and metred poem he will write to thank his hosts,[28] and feeling irritated at the extreme nature of the behaviour he witnesses (especially at the Gate). Spark represents him thinking to himself, 'Why did people have to go to extremes, why couldn't they be moderate?' (*MG*, 11). Barbara, later, at the end of the first chapter, exasperated at what she sees as his lukewarm attitude (he has just expressed a lack of comprehension for why there should be religious obstacles to her marrying Harry Clegg), rebukes him 'in a cold and terrifying voice' (*MG*, 20), quoting a passage from the Apocalypse to him implying that he is 'neither cold nor hot' (*MG*, 21). Freddy's commitment to moderation but not to principle could be read as representing what the Catholic writer is likely to react against in mainstream, Anglican-dominated English society – a valuing of consensus leading to a pragmatic, but not principle-driven, and, possibly, from a Catholic point of view, superficial, approach to moral dilemmas. Freddy could be seen as playing the same role in the novel as Ida Arnold, the Pelagian character, in Graham Greene's *Brighton Rock*, whose arguably superficial understanding of doing good can be interpreted as driving the

---

28 Norman Page, *Muriel Spark* (London: Macmillan, 1990), 58, argues that the rigid metrical forms of Freddy's poetry represent the social rules and conventions he is bound by.

(anti-)hero to his perhaps avoidable doom. Like Barbara, Freddy undergoes a transformation in character during the adventure section of the novel, although for him, unlike Barbara, the effects are strictly temporary.

The Mandelbaum Gate is a novel which offers a solution to, as well as a diagnosis of, the problem of split identity, a solution which is shown as working in the long term for Barbara (though not for Freddy). This solution takes the form of a movement out of the self, in love. For Barbara this takes place at a worldly level, in her love for Harry Clegg, and in her sense of liberation during her adventure in Jordan, but it also has a spiritual dimension, her recognition of a religious dimension which provides a broad framework within which she can escape from personal concerns, although an escape from the self at a worldly level may be necessary to take the step to its spiritual equivalent. The first indication that Barbara is beginning to understand that self-forgetfulness is the way to achieve a unified sense of identity (in contrast to the analysis which we have seen gave her a feeling of disintegration when she was under close questioning by her Polish-Israeli guide) comes on Mount Tabor, where she has driven herself, and on top of which she is presented reflecting on the reminiscences which constitute the bulk of the second chapter, 'Barbara Vaughan's Identity', reminiscences which include her childhood holidays and her recent conversations with Israeli guides. When, looking in the direction of the Dead Sea, where he is working on a dig, she thinks of Harry Clegg, she 'forgot, in her tenderness, that she was a spinster of no fixed identity' (*MG*, 47). Thinking of how he needs her protection owing to his academic absorption, 'She suddenly felt to be insignificant the business of being a Gentile and a Jewess, both and neither, and that of being a wolf in spinster's clothing ...' (*MG*, 47). She imagines how, for different reasons, social (for the Anglican side) and religious-ethnic (for the Jewish side), both sets of her relatives would have been disappointed in her choice, but, 'The point was, he was entirely lovable to her ...' (*MG*, 47). That these reflections strike her on Mount Tabor could be understood as meaning that she is undergoing a kind of transfiguration in her personality, becoming her true self for the first time. Mount Tabor is a traditional site for the Transfiguration.[29]

---

29   Frank Kermode, in 'The Novel as Jerusalem: Muriel Spark's *The Mandelbaum Gate*', *Modern Essays*, Frank Kermode, 2nd edn (London: Fontana, 1971), 276, sees Mount

The principle that movement out of the self unifies the self is illustrated further during the adventure section of the novel, an adventure in which Freddy participates, as well as Barbara. It begins with Barbara entering Jordan in order to visit the many shrines on the Jordanian side of the then border, including those in the Old City of Jerusalem. It is risky for her to enter Jordan because she may be considered to be a spy if she is discovered to have even a partly Jewish background. The danger is exacerbated by the fact that she has been in Israel first, and that she has been interviewed by a journalist in Israel on the subject of a current war-crimes trial; thus there is a possibility of her identity becoming known on the Jordanian side (the article written on her does in fact, when it is released, include the information that she is half-Jewish and is planning to visit Jordan). Freddy, who is already acquainted with Barbara, meets her by chance, on her first day on the Jordanian side, and persuades her that she is in danger, and needs to go into hiding, a plan which he will organize. It is arranged that he will come in the middle of that night to the convent-hostel (called the Convent of St Helena) where she is staying and take her to safety. Barbara imagines this escape from the danger of capture by the Jordanian police as rather 'her escape from the convent' (*MG*, 164), and she even secretly wishes to be caught by the nuns so that she will have the opportunity of explaining that she is not the well-behaved spinster they have taken her for (*MG*, 152–3, 165). Some critics have interpreted this episode as amounting to a rejection of the ideal of the celibate life by Barbara,[30] but later comments by Barbara make it clear that it is her former double life that she is escaping from, in which she appeared to be a confirmed spinster but inwardly was not: she tells Suzi (her guide in Jordan), 'how it now seemed that she had been living like a nun without the intensity and reality of a nun's life' (*MG*, 278). Rodney Stenning Edgecombe describes the life Barbara has been leading before her journey as a 'non-sacramental' celibacy,[31] that is, a life directed inwards, towards herself, and not outwards towards the other, as a nun's or a spouse's would be.

Tabor as representing religious depth behind the modern world, through the idea of the transfiguration of the body.
30 For example, Poitou, 'La rage d'être autre', 20.
31 Edgecombe, *Vocation and Identity*, 84.

Barbara's nocturnal 'escape' from the hostel produces a wave of elation in her, as well as in Freddy, which gives her a sense of having realized her British identity, through having unified the eccentricities inherent in it. Later that night, while in hiding, she imagines the 'good story' she could make of the escape episode, as her Vaughan relatives would (*MG*, 164), and she reflects on how she felt in the car being driven away from the hostel:

> For the first time since her arrival in the Middle East she felt all of a piece; Gentile and Jewess, Vaughan and Aaronson; she had caught some of Freddy's madness, having recognized by his manner in the car, as they careered across Jerusalem, that he had regained some lost or forgotten element in his nature and was now, at last, for some reason, flowering in the full irrational norm of the stock she also derived from: unselfquestioning hierarchists, anarchistic imperialists, blood-sporting zoophiles, sceptical believers – the whole paradoxical lark that had secured, among their bones, the sane life for dead generations of British Islanders. She had caught a bit of Freddy's madness and for the first time in this Holy Land, felt all of a piece, a Gentile Jewess, a private-judging Catholic, a shy adventuress. (*MG*, 164)

This passage, containing phrases understandably much quoted in the critical literature, shows that, on the one hand, she has discovered that an idea of paradox is already a way of understanding British identity, such that the fact that her own self contains oppositions is not incompatible with being British, under this understanding of what Britishness entails. On the other hand the feeling of adventure not only makes sense of the paradoxes inherent in the kind of Britishness she has described, but also allows her to feel that she has pulled her own contradictions into a meaningful whole: not that she has suppressed them, but that they can work together when she moves beyond them into a kind of ecstatic state.

Barbara achieves, in the car, a feeling of unity with Freddy, contrasting with their earlier clash over his lukewarm quality: she responds enthusiastically to his proposals for her to make her pilgrimage in disguise, 'happily making her responses in the dialect of their tribe' (*MG*, 166), the linguistic commonality this time expressing a commonality of feeling, rather than disguising a lack of shared values, as has happened earlier the same day – Freddy, after recognizing Barbara in a shop in the Old City, takes her back, with his English friends, Matt and Joanna, to the villa where they live, and where he regularly stays, in 'A Delightful English Atmosphere'

(*MG*, 51, the title of the third chapter). The relationship between Barbara and the couple starts promisingly, as Barbara jokes and Matt and Joanna laugh, and 'because one always did, in foreign parts, become friendly with one's fellow countrymen more quickly than one did at home' (*MG*, 75). By the end of lunch at the villa, 'they had already formed a small island of mutual Englishness' (*MG*, 75), but this is short-lived, and later on, 'Their island was beginning to disintegrate' (*MG*, 78) as Joanna and Matt think it is 'unfair' for her to risk involving the British Consulate in helping her if she is arrested by the Jordanians for being Jewish, as 'It's a blood-feud between Semites' (*MG*, 78), and therefore not a British problem. It is Freddy, showing the beginnings of the temporary manifestation of spirit which lasts during the Jordanian adventure but not beyond, who defends Barbara's right to consular protection as being the same as any other citizen's, and then rebukes Matt and Joanna for being lukewarm, the same rebuke made to him earlier by Barbara. Thus those British people who have not been seized by an ecstatic spirit will not accept Barbara, with all her background components, as fully British, when they are pressed, and, rather, they force a partial outsider status on her.

Barbara's and Freddy's adventures continue, with Barbara pursuing her pilgrimage in Jordan (including what is now the West Bank), disguised as the servant of Suzi Ramdez, a local young woman, whose family plays a prominent role in the novel. She catches scarlet fever however, and early in the tour has to take cover in Suzi's father's villa, where she convalesces, before continuing her tour. Freddy, at the same time, has a brief affair with Suzi, and discovers a spy ring based at the villa, which is broken up due to his information, but he subsequently forgets what has happened, and even forgets where Barbara is, so that she is lost to outside contact for a period. During the tour of Jordan, after her convalescence, Barbara gives an interesting insight into her world-view, in response to a remark of Suzi's that Barbara talks of profane matters between visits to the sacred places:

> Well, either religious faith penetrates everything in life or it doesn't. There are some experiences which seem to make nonsense of all separations of sacred from profane – they seem childish. Either the whole of life is unified under God or everything falls apart. (*MG*, 283)

For Barbara the religious perspective is a metaphysical umbrella, under which all other aspects of life are ordered and have a meaning: therefore every aspect of life has to be thought about, evaluated, and sometimes re-evaluated, within her overall understanding of spiritual purposes. This world-view of Barbara's gives a clue as to the difference in her reaction to the adventure from Freddy's reaction, as well as to what might seem surprising details in the story of her eventual marriage to Harry Clegg.

Barbara and Freddy are both re-invigorated and enlivened by their Jordanian adventure, but whereas Barbara holds on to the sense of renewal she gains, and does not go back to her former life, Freddy suffers a complete mental block as to what has occurred, later only remembering disconnected snatches, and returns to his former life as if nothing has happened to him. The difference seems to be that Barbara, who has 'the beautiful and dangerous gift of faith' (*MG*, 23), has an overarching framework of ideas and values which is capable of growth, and to which new experiences can be assimilated, whereas Freddy lives according to a set of conventions and habits, which he has not reflected on, and has no way of reconciling them with new, unforeseen experience.[32]

Barbara realizes she cannot marry Harry Clegg according to Church rules unless his previous marriage is annulled, and this possibility is uncertain during her trip. She has decided before the trip that she will not marry him outside the Church (*MG*, 44), but changes her mind once in Israel, and telephones him to tell him (*MG*, 181). She has, with an effort, repented of the affair, but does not regret having fallen in love with him (*MG*, 46). An unlikely train of events leads to Barbara's and Harry's being able to marry in the Church. This involves Miss Rickworth trying to take revenge on her by forging a birth certificate for Harry according to which he was baptized Catholic. She believes this will make it impossible for him to obtain an annulment, but the contrary is the case. Although Barbara's being a committed Catholic, yet being prepared to marry Harry outside the Church (while we do not know if she would in fact have done it),

---

32   Allan Massie, *Muriel Spark* (Edinburgh: Ramsey Head, 1979), 65, suggests that Freddy is like an enlightened pagan, such as Dante's Virgil.

seems to be a contradiction, there are indications that Barbara herself is aware that it would be unlikely to have worked as a long-term arrangement – she tells him, 'I would have married you, anyway. But it would have taken courage to continue being out of the Church. It's the keeping it up I was afraid of' (*MG*, 244). She then adds, 'With God everything is possible' (*MG*, 244). This statement could be interpreted as an assertion that Divine Providence has intervened on behalf of Barbara, rewarding her for her generous impulse.[33] Her eventual marriage is described, close to the end of the novel, in low-key terms: 'Barbara and Harry were married and got on fairly well together ever after' (*MG*, 303). This description seems an anticlimax, but the context for understanding it may be seen in the earlier account of her (sacramental) confession to a priest of her affair, before her journey, when she tries to excuse herself by telling him 'It was a love-affair' and he replies 'Yes, well, don't pretend it was the Beatific Vision' (*MG*, 46). What this exchange indicates, in harmony with other indications as to Barbara's evolving world-view, as well as the framework within which Spark herself is presenting the events, is that Barbara's love for Harry takes its meaning from within the larger spiritual purposes of Barbara's life. Therefore Barbara's love for Harry is important, as it takes her out of herself, and is a step on a road of spiritual development, taking her in a divine direction.

Jerusalem in particular, and the Holy Land in general, as well as standing for Barbara's divisions, are also an example of how an overarching spiritual identity can provide a framework within which divisions can be reconciled, in the identity of a place in the same way as in a human personality, such as Barbara's. Barbara, early in the novel, has been resistant to seeing different elements of the history of places she has visited as consonant, wanting to dissociate biblical places from their modern manifestations. For example, she clashes with one of the Israeli guides over Beer Sheva, insisting, when she is shown modern Beer Sheva, 'I'm really only interested in the Beersheba of Genesis', to which the guide responds,

---

33 Caporaletti, *A World in a Grain of Sand*, 300, believes that Providence rewards Barbara for her spirit of independence.

'This is the Beersheba of Genesis' (*MG*, 23–4). Discussing what she wants to see on her journey, she also tells her friend, Saul Ephraim, 'I'm really interested essentially in the Holy Land', eliciting the response, 'This is the Holy Land' (*MG*, 24). While she is in the Old City, already in disguise, but beginning to suffer from the effects of scarlet fever, so that she is not listening, she attends a Mass in the Church of the Holy Sepulchre during which an English priest gives a sermon explaining the relationship between the Jerusalem of history and the spiritual Jerusalem:

> Jerusalem has been in many hands. Then, as now, soldiers patrolled the Holy Land. Jerusalem has been destroyed, rebuilt, fought over, conquered, and now is divided again. (*MG*, 199)

Here, the parallels between the Jerusalem of Barbara's present and of biblical times are similar to those drawn by Jones and Waugh. The priest explains that 'The historical evidence of our faith is scattered about under the ground' (*MG*, 199), but that this lack of tidiness gives faith its role, faith which will no longer be necessary 'When we have come to perfection in time' (*MG*, 199). The priest explains further:

> For there is a supernatural process going on under the surface and within the substance of all things. In the Jerusalem of history we see the type and shadow of that Jerusalem of Heaven that St John of Patmos tells of in the Apocalypse ... This is the spiritual city that is involved eternally with the historical one. It is the city of David, the city of God's people in exile; 'If I forget thee, O Jerusalem, let my tongue cleave to the roof of my mouth; if I prefer not Jerusalem above my chief joy'. It is the city of Jesus, not only of his death, but of his rising again alive. It is the New Jerusalem which we seek with our faith, and which is the goal of our pilgrimage to this old Jerusalem of history. 'What is faith?' said St Paul. 'It is that which gives substance to our hopes, which convinces us of things we cannot see'. (*MG*, 199)

This sermon could be regarded as representing Spark's view, and the dynamic of the historical and spiritual identities can readily be transferred to the realm of individual personality, but it also recalls famous theories of spiritual and earthly cities: apart from the heavenly and historical Jerusalem of the Old and New Testament, the heavenly and earthly Cities of Rome in St Augustine's *City of God* may be brought to mind. The essential pattern

Muriel Spark: Layers of Identity

of the idea is that, while the spiritual city is the goal, the earthly city is a necessary step on the journey. The earthly Jerusalem was necessary as the scene for many of the biblical events, and the earthly Rome was needed as the historical basis for the spread of Christianity round the Mediterranean world, and then beyond. The historical role leads towards a spiritual goal, but the history remains the narrative, a necessary part of the understanding of what is being achieved. In addition, given that from a Catholic point of view the human being is always composed of a soul and a body, even after the Resurrection, physical, historical human realities are on the one hand ultimately transcended, but on the other hand taken up into the transcendent state. The sermon makes it clear that, as Spark understands it, a process of movement, which in the sermon is the element of faith, is what allows disparate elements to become entwined and form a whole. It is as part of a narrative, with a goal, that disparate components, the physical and spiritual levels of reality, or separate and sometimes conflicting histories and cultures, can be woven together, whereas from a static point of view only the separation is seen.

During her pilgrimage Barbara finds that she is in a minority as a Christian, on both the Israeli and the Jordanian sides of the border, and her guides are either not particularly interested in showing her Christian shrines (in Israel) or have a superficial knowledge of Christian shrines for professional reasons but no deeper interest (Suzi in Jordan). In the Church of the Holy Sepulchre there is even interdenominational rivalry between Christians, and the quiet Catholic Mass is drowned out by the more musical Orthodox Mass at the neighbouring altar. The minority status of Catholics in the Holy Land is part of what makes the Holy Land a good model for how Barbara can understand living as a Catholic in Britain. It has not been necessary for her to go to a Catholic country to make, for her, a faith-affirming and -renewing journey, and the religious significance of the Holy Land for Catholics is not diminished by the space being shared with people of many religions and none, who in fact have a necessary place in the evolving history of the land, including its history seen from a Catholic transcendental point of view.

There is an interesting oblique allusion to a philosophical position relevant to Barbara's world-view, at the point where Barbara recalls Miss

Rickworth, her former housemate, discussing 'the doctrine that existence precedes essence' (*MG*, 154). Barbara, in Israel, remembering, doubts whether Miss Rickworth could have found any application for this idea 'to the world she existed in' (*MG*, 154), but it is arguable that Barbara, during the course of the novel, does find an application for a similar principle. The existentialist language used by Miss Rickworth is different from, but not inconsistent with, a Catholic Balthasarian philosophy in which essence is understood as a movement out of the self.[34] Thus Barbara's discussions on secular philosophy with Miss Rickworth are another element in her background which she does not have to discard, but can integrate in her developing world-view.

In *The Mandelbaum Gate* then Spark arguably works out and articulates the solution to the problems of fitting together the disparate elements of her religious and national background, represented in the person of Barbara (as well as solving other splits in Barbara's personality, which may have been real for Spark as well). These splits in national and religious background were described in *Curriculum Vitae* and 'The Gentile Jewesses', but the solution was not laid out. Given that Spark mentions her conversion, in *Curriculum Vitae*, in the context of her extensive reading of Newman leading up to it, it is not surprising that a Newmanian shape to her representation of how personal conflicts of identity can be resolved is discernible. Just as Newman did not need to discard or disown his Anglican inheritance in order to become Catholic, but could rather see it as pointing in the direction which he eventually took, Spark, looking back, creates a narrative for her alter ego, Barbara, in which Barbara's (Anglican) Protestant and Jewish sides together, and perhaps also individually, point her towards the religious journey which she takes. Substituting Spark herself for Barbara, and reading *The Mandelbaum Gate* together with 'The Gentile Jewesses', we can see that for Spark, her somewhat vague Jewish and (undefined) Protestant religious background does not, for her, stand in opposition to her Catholic conversion, but rather leads to it. In the light of the overarching

---

34 Hans Urs von Balthasar, *Epilogue*, trans. by Edward T. Oakes (San Francisco: Ignatius, 2004).

spiritual narrative which is clearly established as the ultimate framework of reference in *The Mandelbaum Gate*, considerations of nationality are of secondary importance, but their importance is not effaced, because of the dual spiritual and physical nature of the human being from the book's perspective. From the perspective of the spiritual narrative, the cultural and social contexts which the individual passes through are all part of how the individual reaches his or her spiritual destination, and derive their importance from their ineradicable place in that narrative. The place of archaeology in the novel (in the form of Harry Clegg's profession) suggests the way that each part of a place's or person's identity is permanently present, constituting how the person or place has come to be what he, she or it is. The particular emphasis of the novel, which is consonant with the emphases of recent (for example, Balthasarian) Catholic philosophy, is that it is through coming out of the self (in love) that the self, moving towards its purpose, can create its story, as part of which all the elements which have gone into forming it fall into place.

A Holy Land in which Christians are a minority, but which is full of places of Christian significance, and in which the presence of non-Christians has been necessary for its Christian story to unfold, can be compared to, and may be intended to parallel, a Britain in which Catholics are a minority, but which is full of places of Catholic significance, and in which recent Catholic history (such as Newman's conversion, and his subsequent important contributions to Catholic thinking) depends on the presence of non-Catholics – although this parallel is not drawn out in the novel. Nevertheless Barbara's finding that she can fit her experience in the Holy Land into her spiritual narrative, interacting fruitfully with people of different religions on the way, is followed by her returning to England, marrying the (in practice) non-Catholic Harry, and having a child with him. In an understated way, like Waugh's Guy Crouchback, she has found her way back to a place in British society, while retaining her Catholic identity, but responding to difference with love.

CHAPTER 4

Alternative Approaches: G. K. Chesterton and Graham Greene

During the twentieth century, especially the early and middle years, a number of prominent Catholic writers were active in Britain, and it is arguably a time when Catholics were more prominent in British literature than might be expected given their status as a fairly small minority within the population. In this chapter Chesterton and Greene, two important British Catholic writers of the period, will be discussed with a view to illuminating the wider literary context in which Jones, Waugh and Spark were working. Chesterton and Greene, though concerned with both national and religious identity, do not approach these issues through the perspective of that integrative theory of identity which we have seen to be characteristic of Jones, Waugh and Spark. Thus they are introduced here as a kind of 'control' case, to show that the approach taken by the other three is a distinctive perspective, and that some Catholics wrote about the same themes of national and religious identity without seeking to resolve the conflicts they discovered by recourse to the developing Catholic theory of traditions. As both Chesterton and Greene wrote many works in which issues of national and religious identity feature, and as both were prolific writers, the focus here will be on a limited selection of works which illustrate the position of each writer with respect to the themes. The chapter will argue that although Greene does recognize that there is a clash between British and Catholic identities, he does not address the problem of how the clash might be resolved. Chesterton, on the other hand, does not thematize the clash, and at the same time subscribes to a kind of Romantic theory of nationalism, in which national identities are discrete entities – thus the mixing and layering, which is part of how Jones, Waugh and Spark all envisage conflicts of identity being resolved, is not readily compatible with Chesterton's vision.

G. K. Chesterton

G. K. Chesterton was born in London in 1874, so belongs to a generation earlier than the other writers who feature in this study, but his literary activity overlaps with the careers of Jones, Waugh and Greene. He was of an English middle-class family, although his mother had a French maiden name, which may have derived, as he writes, from a French prisoner of war in England, captured during the wars following the French Revolution, and her mother was Scottish – and he claims in his autobiography to have had a kind of romantic attachment to this Scottish connection during his childhood.[1] He was baptized into the Church of England, but his maternal grandfather had been a Methodist lay preacher (*AGKC*, 21, 29). However he hints indirectly that his childhood home, like Victorian homes generally, was rather secularized compared with the homes of previous generations (*AGKC*, 36). He converted to the Catholic Church in 1922,[2] having been an Anglo-Catholic for some time before that (and experiencing a youthful crisis, during which he had not been religious at all, and had experimented with various non-religious ideas and philosophies),[3] so much of his writing with a Catholic slant pre-dates his conversion. During his career in journalism, literature and controversy, Chesterton was closely associated with his friend, Hilaire Belloc, another Catholic writer, who was Anglo-French, and to whom Chesterton held similar views on many issues.

---

1   G. K. Chesterton, *The Autobiography of G. K. Chesterton* (San Francisco: Ignatius, 2006) (*AGKC*), 22, 29. Further references to this edition are given after quotations in the text. For Chesterton's ancestry see also Michael Coren, *Gilbert: The Man Who Was G. K. Chesterton* (London: Jonathan Cape, 1989), 7–10, according to whom Chesterton's mother's French surname was due to her being descended from an exile from French-speaking Switzerland.
2   See Dudley Barker, *G. K. Chesterton: A Biography* (London: Constable, 1973), 249. For more on Chesterton's biography, see also Ian Ker, *G. K. Chesterton: A Biography* (Oxford: Oxford University Press, 2011).
3   This youthful crisis is noted, for example, by Lee Oser, *The Return of Christian Humanism: Chesterton, Eliot, Tolkien, and the Romance of History* (Columbia: University of Missouri Press, 2007), 21.

Chesterton broached the theme of nationality in a substantial way in his early novel, *The Napoleon of Notting Hill*, first published in 1904. It thus appeared long before he joined the Catholic Church. It is not about religious identity but was written as an expression of local patriotism, and anti-imperialism.[4] In *The Autobiography* Chesterton includes a chapter on the novel, in which he situates it in the context of the controversy over the Boer War, during which Chesterton sympathized with the Boer cause (*AGKC*, 109–32). In the novel, set in a future time, different suburbs of London become independent states, and battles are fought between them in a chivalrous fashion, reminiscent of the Middle Ages. That Chesterton values the local places him close to Jones, but his vision of local patriotism as it appears in this novel is a Romantic one, in contrast to Jones, who theorizes the mixing and layering of cultures, and shows no interest in their separating out into warring units. While the vision of London boroughs at war with each other may have been an exaggeration of the situation he would have liked to see in reality, Chesterton does appear to have believed in the salutary nature of fighting, if of a non-mechanized kind, a view not found in Jones' works. Jones is rather concerned with how to make sense of suffering and sacrifice, and clearly sees the enmity between Western European peoples, which he experienced in the First World War, as calamitous.[5]

Perhaps Chesterton's best known literary project is constituted by the Father Brown Stories, the first volume of which, *The Innocence of Father*

---

4   For Chesterton's emphasis on local loyalty, see P. J. Kavanagh, 'Chesterton Reappraised', *G. K. Chesterton: Half a Century of Views*, D. J. Conlon, ed. (Oxford: Oxford University Press, 1987), 356, while Alison Milbank, *Chesterton and Tolkien as Theologians: The Fantasy of the Real* (London: T & T Clark, 2007), 8, points out that he (like Tolkien) was not an imperialist. For the insight that Chesterton's belief in local patriotism is linked to his conviction that frames and limits are beneficial, see William Oddie, *Chesterton and the Romance of Orthodoxy: The Making of GKC 1874–1908* (Oxford: Oxford University Press, 2008), 264.

5   Michael D. Hurley, *G. K. Chesterton* (Tavistock: Northcote, 2012), 51, notes that Chesterton could be against war, for example, when it was for imperialistic purposes, and also objected to some kinds of journalistic pro-war rhetoric, such as comparing war to sport.

Brown, was published in 1911, though there were four more volumes, and he continued writing these stories throughout the rest of his literary career.[6] They are detective stories in which the detective is a Catholic priest. They were started long before Chesterton's conversion, and the detective priest, Father Brown, was modelled on a Catholic priest, Father John O'Connor, who was a friend of Chesterton's. Father O'Connor was Irish but Chesterton transforms him into an English Catholic priest for the stories.[7] In the first piece in the series, 'The Blue Cross', when Father Brown is being introduced, Chesterton does his best to make Father Brown as English as possible, describing him as unexotic, and presenting him as being from eastern England, which is as far from Ireland and as uncomplicatedly English as can be imagined, since it was a region which had relatively little Irish immigration due to the Industrial Revolution. In his later book *Irish Impressions*[8] he writes that 'the determining part' of his own ancestry is English from East Anglia, 'at the flattest and farthest extreme from the Celtic fringe' (*II*, 82). Father Brown is first encountered on a train from Harwich to London, which he has boarded in 'a small Essex village' (*IFB*, 9), and he is observed by a French detective on the train: 'The little priest was so much the essence of those Eastern flats: he had a face as round and dull as a Norfolk dumpling; he had eyes as empty as the North Sea; he had several brown-paper parcels which he was quite incapable of collecting'. (*IFB*, 9) The commonplace English person (observed by a flamboyant French character), who happens to be a Catholic priest, seems designed to assure the reader that a Catholic priest can be an absolutely English personality, with nothing exotic about him. Representing the Catholic priest as completely and ordinarily English may be an attempt to prevent the English reader from reacting to the idea of a Catholic priest as neces-

---

6   G. K. Chesterton, *The Innocence of Father Brown* (London: Penguin, 1950) (*IFB*). Further references to this edition are given after quotations in the text.
7   On Father O'Connor as the inspiration for Father Brown, see for example Joseph Pearce, *Wisdom and Innocence: A Life of G. K. Chesterton* (London: Hodder and Stoughton, 1996), 92–3.
8   G. K. Chesterton, *Irish Impressions* (Norfolk, VA: IHS Press, 2002) (*II*). Further references to this edition are given after quotations in the text.

sarily something exotic or foreign. To this extent Chesterton's intention is perhaps similar to Waugh's, when he tries to persuade the reader of *Helena* that Helena's empirical hard-headedness is a characteristic shared by British people and Catholic theology, such that British people ought to be able to be Catholics without sacrificing their identity. Chesterton, however, in his work generally, does not make a point of contrasting Englishness with Catholic identity, so the issue of how they can be reconciled does not arise. To the extent that there is a contrast in identities elaborated in 'The Blue Cross', for example, it is between the Frenchness of the detective, Valentin, who has an explicit, abstract rational explanation for all his procedures, including his reliance on chance in looking for clues, and Father Brown, who in an empirical English fashion relies on observation of detail, and on encyclopaedic knowledge of criminal tricks, derived from what he has learnt from penitents. On the other hand, the French criminal, Flambeau, displays a French speculative bent, in suggesting that there might be another kind of reason on other planets (during a conversation with Father Brown), whereas Father Brown defends the Catholic position, that reason would always be the same reason on any planet (*IFB*, 24–5).[9] As the position that reason is always the same may seem to coincide with the notion of British hard-headed common sense, as contrasted with French, or continental, speculative reason, Father Brown in this case again effortlessly combines Britishness with Catholicism, and no conflict between the two, requiring resolution, arises.

Chesterton had strong views on English history, which fed into his political philosophy, distributism, and his account of the country's history is summarized in the brief book *A Short History of England*,[10] first published in 1917, although it is a subject he alludes to frequently across his writings. His understanding of this history is based on the conviction that

---

[9] William Wallace Robson, 'Father Brown and Others', *G. K. Chesterton: A Centenary Appraisal* (London: Paul Elek, 1974), 67, notices that in never denying reason Father Brown is true both to Catholic theology and to the tradition of the genre of detective fiction.

[10] G. K. Chesterton, *A Short History of England* (Teddington: Echo Library, 2008) (*SHE*). Further references to this edition are given after quotations in the text.

England is an oligarchy, and that the oligarchy took power as a result of the dissolution of the monasteries and the redistribution of the monasteries' property to private owners, who, unlike the monasteries, did not understand their ownership as holding the property for the benefit of the population at large. He is also keen to counter the contention of 'Teutonists' that the pre-Anglo-Saxon population of the area which became England was largely replaced by Germanic peoples, insisting rather on continuity in the population (*SHE*, 17–18), as he equally insists on a Roman element in British identity (*SHE*, 7) – that the First World War was still in progress is no doubt relevant to the pro-Roman and anti-Teutonic leaning being expressed. Chesterton in this book, as in his writings more generally, gives different nationalities discrete and stable characters. So, for example, towards the beginning of the work he describes the peoples of Britain and Ireland as characterized by 'insecurity', due to their inhabiting islands, an insecurity which manifests itself in terms of 'confusion of speech' in the case of the Irish and 'confusion of thought' in the case of the English. He attributes this characteristic (insecurity) to all the British and Irish nationalities, despite conceding that the four nationalities are different from each other, and sees this characteristic as separating the British and Irish nationalities from others, such as the Germans and French, who have their own characters. Rather than examine a changing and accumulating culture, Chesterton thinks in terms of 'the English soul' (*SHE*, 102), a way of understanding nationality akin to that of nineteenth-century Romanticism.[11]

Chesterton, while supporting English patriotism, also expressed himself in favour of other patriotisms, including those of nationalities which had found themselves under English domination, and he voiced his support for Irish patriotism in his book *Irish Impressions*, first published in 1919. He argues that Ireland is home to a 'European peasantry' and therefore cannot be ruled by England, as English people do not understand the

---

11   See also Chesterton's poem 'The Rolling English Road', which sings of the English characteristic of creating winding roads, dating back to before Roman times, as the poem asserts. G. K. Chesterton, *The Collected Poems of G. K. Chesterton* (London: Methuen, 1950), 203.

system which Irish people would put in place if they were able, a system very different from the oligarchy he believes England to be (*II*, 37–8). He views nationalism as a positive phenomenon, because it is what prevents imperialism (*II*, 86), but he sees the Celticism present in some kinds of Irish nationalism of his time as exaggerated (*II*, 85–8). Towards the end of the book, he voices his conviction that a nation exists in the same way that persons do, and that the Irish, English and French are all clearly nations (*II*, 110) – he has illustrated one way in which the distinction between the English and Irish nations can be identified by discussing the different ways in which the English language is used by each nation (*II*, 107–8). So once again, what emerges is an understanding of nations as discrete units, and Chesterton does not recognize any difficulty in determining which groups constitute nations.

Chesterton wrote the biography *Geoffrey Chaucer*[12] late in his career – it was first published in 1932. It reflects extensively on what Englishness is. Early in the work he states that the English are eccentrics (*GC*, 1), credits Chaucer with being in some way the father of the English nation (*GC*, 1–20), and later repeats his contention that the English nation would become characterized by its oligarchy after the Reformation (*GC*, 19). In the sixth chapter, 'Chaucer as an Englishman', Chesterton explains his position on the state of the English nation at the time of Chaucer in these terms: 'We can say that the Englishman was emergent' (*GC*, 106). He describes the type of the English man (or 'gentleman') as it appeared in the eighteenth century, and is still current at his time, which involves being practical and unemotional, and derives from puritanism and industrialism, and goes on to suggest that the English of Chaucer's time would have been without any such characteristics and would have been more like what later English people would have regarded as continental (*GC*, 107). He explains how this would be the case partly by arguing that the English and the French were almost one nation at around Chaucer's time, and that the 'national types' were very close to each other then (*GC*, 108). Interestingly he insists that

---

12 G. K. Chesterton, *Geoffrey Chaucer* (London: House of Stratus, 2000) (*GC*). Further references to this edition are given after quotations in the text.

the English person of Chaucer's time would not have had a self-image as 'a plain blunt Englishman' (*GC*, 108) – this contrasts with Waugh's portrayal of Helena as possessing a no-nonsense British empirical attitude, but it has to be borne in mind that this empiricism may be one of the deliberate anachronisms that Waugh, in his preface, admitted to using as a literary device. Chesterton details a series of loyalties which a European person of Chaucer's time would have felt – feudal, imperial and, most importantly, religious (*GC*, 108). He argues though that the beginnings of modern national consciousness were already subconsciously present in Chaucer, and can be seen in various ways in his life and work. Examples include his contentment with being moderately successful and doing practical work alongside his literary career, his ability to get on with others and tendency to avoid contentious issues, and his sense of humour akin to a sense of adventure for its own sake (this humour being a characteristic which puritanism and public-school culture, both despised by Chesterton, have been unable to destroy); the Prioress displays characteristics of the English lady, such as in her love of animals; Chaucer shows English individualism, and suggests that England is characterised by a personal quality, rather than a principle, like other nationalities (*GC*, 109–23).

Chesterton's position on English national identity in *Geoffrey Chaucer* is more sophisticated and nuanced than his position as expressed in the earlier works discussed above. He recognizes that English national identity has evolved, places less emphasis on the idea that it has always been in some way the same, and even suggests that it had not yet really formed at Chaucer's time. He draws attention to a variety of influences that have shaped modern English identity, and presents a picture in which vestiges of earlier influences more or less survive the overlay of later influences, sometimes hostile to the earlier. Chesterton in this work makes explicit his view that Protestantism (in the form of puritanism) has shaped modern English identity, such that the development of English culture would have taken a different course if the Reformation had not taken place. He does not, however, examine the question, which might arise from this analysis, as to how a modern English person could be simultaneously English and Catholic – this question would not in any case have arisen in the context of a biography of Chaucer.

Chesterton's understanding of national identity, despite its growth in complexity as seen in *Geoffrey Chaucer*, is always characterized by a search for the essence of particular national identities. He does not think in terms of an accumulation of cultural deposits, as does Jones, nor in terms of accumulations of influences in personal histories, as do Waugh and Spark, and his interest appears to be in what each national identity is, rather than in the question of their continuing development.

Graham Greene

Graham Greene, who was born in Berkhamsted in 1904, was a contemporary and friend of Waugh, and like all the authors discussed in this study was a convert to Catholicism, converting in 1926 (received in February 1926), as a consequence of an investigation into Catholicism motivated by meeting his future wife, Vivien.[13] Both his parents were English and they were cousins, and the Greene family was a family connected with East Anglia.[14] Unlike the other writers considered here, Greene's relationship with the Catholic Church appeared to weaken as he became older, a situation which led his friend Waugh, at one stage, to conclude that he had lost his faith altogether.[15] While he became estranged from his wife,[16] and replaced her with other female companions, and while some of his books explored protagonists in difficult relations to the Church, as well as addressing issues concerning doubt and faith, he never formally left the

---

13   See Graham Greene, *A Sort of Life* (London: Vintage, 1999), 118–21.
14   For Greene's birth and parentage see Norman Sherry, *The Life of Graham Greene*, 3 vols (London: Jonathan Cape, 1989–2004), vol. 1, 3–4.
15   See Waugh, *The Diaries of Evelyn Waugh*, 779 and Graham Greene, *A Life in Letters*, Richard Greene, ed. (London: Abacus, 2007), 251.
16   For the break-up with Vivien see, for example, Michael Shelden, *Graham Greene: The Man Within* (London: Heinemann, 1994), 274–9.

Church, and in his late years spent much time with a friend who was a priest (Father Leopoldo Durán), who said daily Mass for him.[17]

Greene's novels frequently portray English men who are expatriates, and he often sets them in countries which he was himself drawn to, particularly in Latin America (for example, *The Power and the Glory* in Mexico, *Our Man in Havana* in Cuba and *The Honorary Consul* in Argentina and Paraguay). Greene in his own life moved away from England, and lived mainly abroad, especially in France and French-speaking Switzerland. However, despite the fact that the English person attracted to foreign, often Catholic, countries, is a frequent protagonist in the novels, and that many, though not all, of his novels make Catholicism an important theme, Greene does not usually focus on the compatibility or otherwise of Catholic and English, or British, identities. The interaction and clash between these does arise prominently however in *Brighton Rock*.[18]

Brighton Rock (1938) narrates the relationship between Pinkie, a young criminal and gang member living in Brighton, and his girlfriend, Rose. Pinkie is involved in a murder early in the novel, and Ida Arnold, a woman who suspects him, tracks him down, in a pursuit during which, in his attempt to evade capture, he commits further crimes, including murder, and eventually kills himself. Pinkie and Rose, young people from poor backgrounds in a Catholic area of Brighton, form a running contrast with Ida, a Londoner and non-Catholic, throughout the novel.[19] Pinkie is a former choirboy, and, though lapsed, is proud of his Catholic identity, and of being different from non-Catholics. He subscribes to a bleak religious vision, which critics have identified as having Manichean, or Jansenist features.[20] The novel emphasizes how both Pinkie and Rose, because of their Catholic background and despite their differences, understand the world in a different way from the majority view in their society. They believe in

---

17   See Sherry, *The Life of Graham Greene*, vol. 3, 661–81.
18   Graham Greene, *Brighton Rock* (London: Vintage, 2004) (*BR*). Further references to this edition are given after quotations in the text.
19   Roger Sharrock, *Saints, Sinners and Comedians: The Novels of Graham Greene* (Tunbridge Wells: Burns and Oates, 1984), 82, for example, notes this contrast.
20   See, for example, David Lodge, *Graham Greene* (New York: Columbia University Press, 1966), 8, 20–1.

a spiritual reality and accept that this reality can be reasoned about. In particular, they have an acute sense of good and evil. In contrast to them the majority society is complacent, lacking in clarity on existential issues, and is devoid of a sense of good and evil. The chief representative of the Pelagian majority view is Ida, who thinks in terms of right and wrong, rather than of good and evil, thus in terms of categories which, from Greene's point of view, are conventional, bearing no necessary connection with spiritual and moral realities. The figure of Ida splits the critics: some view her as the heroine of the novel, while others see her as a major, or even the chief, target of Greene's criticism and disdain.[21] There are, however, indications in the novel that point to the likelihood that Ida's character, and the secular world-view she represents,[22] are not shared or endorsed by Greene – these indications are separate from the difficult issue of how to evaluate Ida's seeking justice against Pinkie, and pushing him towards further crime and suicide in the process. For example, Ida is presented as superstitious, in contrast to Rose and Pinkie, who stand out for the clarity of their thinking and their lack of sentimentality, and the Anglican funeral of Hale, Pinkie's first victim, is portrayed as lacking in depth.[23] More profoundly, it has been noted that Ida is a character who is incapable of love and commitment to another person, and is only capable of temporary attachments, in contrast to Rose, who embodies the principle of love.[24] David Lodge argues that Greene is asserting the Baudelairian paradox,

---

21   On Ida, see for example Richard Johnstone, *The Will to Believe: Novelists of the Nineteen-thirties* (Oxford: Oxford University Press, 1982), 73, who sees Ida as taking on the role of fate, but without the basis of adequate values (this is a course of action perhaps reminiscent of Miss Jean Brodie), or Sharrock, *Saints, Sinners and Comedians*, 94–9, who associates Ida with qualities such as complacency and self-righteousness, and a humanistic conviction that she knows what is best for others. Michael G. Brennan, *Graham Greene: Fictions, Faith and Authorship* (London: Continuum, 2010), 3, by contrast, describes Ida as 'the novel's most potent force for good'.
22   David Lodge, *Graham Greene*, 21, notes that Ida represents secular values.
23   Cedric Watts, *Darkest Greeneland: Brighton Rock* (Berkhamsted: Graham Greene Birthplace Trust, 1999), 10–11, argues that lukewarm attitudes are presented as worse than evil in the novel, and points out that Hale's Anglican funeral is satirized.
24   See, for example, Alan Price, *Brighton Rock (Graham Greene)* (Oxford: Blackwell, 1969), 82.

that good and evil have more in common with each other than either has with Ida's conventional code of right and wrong, but it is also possible that Greene distorts Catholic principles in order to make this point, a point intended to shock his readers, and Lodge suggests, as others do, that Greene had recourse to Manichean or Jansenist, rather than orthodox Catholic, principles.[25] It is hard to discern whether Greene's purpose in the novel is to highlight a problem of national identity: the Catholic characters are a minority in a culture dominated by Protestant or secular post-Protestant values, but, as Lodge points out, Greene often works with a 'fruitful tension between two systems of value'.[26] *Brighton Rock* does not raise the question as to whether Pinkie and Rose, as a members of a cultural minority, can be fully English, or British, so the question of how they could reconcile their Catholic identity with a fully English, or British, identity, does not arise, as it does for Guy Crouchback.

Chesterton and Greene both write about Catholicism, and about nationality, but they place less stress on the problematic relationship between Catholicism and Britishness, or Englishness, Scottishness and Welshness, than do Jones, Waugh and Spark, and they do not thematize the reconciliation between identities by means of blending and development of traditions that we have noted in the other writers' work. A consideration of Chesterton and Greene's writing indicates that the specific integrating theory espoused by Jones, Waugh and Spark is not an inevitable aspect of the writing of all Catholic British authors of the twentieth century, and that questions of Catholic and British identity are not necessarily central in these authors' works, but that there is a recurrent interest in them, which produces a range of literary responses.

---

25   Lodge, *Graham Greene*, 8, 20–1. Sharrock, *Saints, Sinners and Comedians*, 91, 98, for example, complains of Greene's Jansenism in *Brighton Rock*. Brennan, *Graham Greene*, 4 argues that Greene used Manichean or Jansenist ideas for his fictional purposes, without subscribing to them himself.
26   Lodge, *Graham Greene*, 18.

Conclusion

David Jones, Evelyn Waugh and Muriel Spark, in the texts discussed here, all address the issue of what it is to be Catholic in a non-Catholic Britain, and of whether Britishness and Catholicism can coincide harmoniously. There are differences, as well as striking similarities, between the writers' approaches, but, in particular, I have been arguing that all three use conceptual resources available to them in the Catholic tradition to find a way of affirming the possibility of being both Catholic and at home in Britain, despite the degree of conflict between Catholicism and majority British culture which all three acknowledge. They are involved in a project of reconciliation, a project which can reach beyond reconciling Catholic and British identity, to reconcile other components within British society with which the writers are familiar – Welsh and English identity for Jones, and Jewish and non-Jewish identity for Spark.

Since the fiction and non-fiction discussed above appeared in the early and mid-twentieth century, the writers are addressing a cultural balance which is different from that obtaining in the early twenty-first century, to the extent that the majority culture in relation to which Jones, Waugh and Spark's Catholicism is a minority culture is clearly a Protestant culture, albeit one exhibiting signs of secularization – Anglican in England, Presbyterian in Scotland, and a Nonconformist/Anglican mixture in Wales. Had they been writing a few decades later, they would have been facing a majority British culture with a more diffuse religious identity, in a country with a greater number of prominent minorities; thus the position of Catholics as the Other 'par excellence', as Poitou puts it, might have been less evident.

Waugh and Spark show particularly strong similarity with each other, in that they focus on individuals, and their protagonists at least partially represent their biographical selves, and face personal conflicts of identity: the protagonists solve the conflicts by means of moving from states of reflection to states of action, involving interaction with others and fulfilling providentially allotted tasks (finding the True Cross for Helena, and creating a family for Guy and Barbara). Particularly in the case of *Sword of Honour* and *The Mandelbaum Gate*, characters of Waugh's and Spark's own time (Guy and Barbara) confront conflicts of identity, including the issue of how to be Catholic in non-Catholic Britain, but also face further divisions within their identity (English versus Italian for Guy, Jewish versus Gentile for Barbara), and find a way, ultimately, to transcend these conflicts by focusing on outward-looking action, a stance which allows them to find a place in British society by the end of the narrative. To the extent that Guy and Barbara closely correspond to Waugh and Spark, it is interesting to note that, of the characters' creators, Waugh emulated Guy by finding his place in England, and living in country houses in the West Country with a large family (larger than Guy's, who, we are told, only has the one stepson). Spark, however, was already divorced by the time her writing career began, with a son who was looked after by her parents, and after a precarious professional life in London, in later life she moved to and settled in Italy, never to marry again – thus not emulating Barbara's domestically fruitful homecoming.

Jones, in contrast to Waugh and Spark, does not for the most part tackle the Catholic-British and English-Welsh conflicts of identity through the fictional investigation of the psychology of well-defined individuals, but rather explores the culture at large, gathering varied cultural references, and looking for as deep a historical perspective as possible. The character John Ball in *In Parenthesis* is his only contemporary protagonist, and he is a pair of eyes and ears, rather than a consciousness explored in depth. He only appears during the period of the First World War during which the action takes place, with no indication as to his past or future (and he is not a Catholic, although references to Catholics are present). It is arguable that for Jones an awareness of the history of Britain, with its many centuries of Catholic heritage, in itself solves the difficulty of understanding the individual's place in modern Britain as a Catholic.

Conclusion

As Aidan Nichols has suggested is the case with British Catholic writers,[1] Jones, Waugh and Spark all have a strong tendency to distinguish between English, Welsh and Scottish identities. Jones is especially consistent in this respect, and sees the distinction between Welsh and English identities as being related to the problem of the recovery of Catholic culture in Britain, to the extent that, as he presents it, Welsh culture, though not now Catholic, has a longer memory than popular English culture; thus English culture, were it to learn from Welsh culture to look further into the past than the Reformation, would recover an awareness of its Catholic past, together with other elements of its history. Spark, despite explicitly discussing conflicts between Scottish and English culture in her autobiography, *Curriculum Vitae*, simplifies, in *The Mandelbaum Gate*, her protagonist's conflicts in comparison with her own by removing the Scottish element and making Barbara English (Jewish and non-Jewish). Waugh, despite acknowledging strains of Scottish and Welsh (and Irish and Huguenot) ancestry in himself (far enough in the past to preclude direct influence on his growing up), writes about English protagonists, Guy Crouchback's national complication coming from his having grown up partly in Italy. There is, however, an important recognition, in *Helena*, of the way that Welsh culture underlies English culture, and Helena is presented as British in the ancient sense (British Celtic), at the same time as, from the point of view of the anachronistic imposition of modern identities, Welshness and Englishness seem to be present in her.

Both Jones and Waugh, when they do think in terms of Britishness, often associate the notion with the British Empire, and the parallel between the Roman and British empires is drawn by all three writers: Spark makes it fleetingly in *The Mandelbaum Gate*, Waugh makes it the basis of the novel *Helena*, and it constitutes a fundamental recurrent element in Jones' work. Jones and Waugh both also draw the parallel between the Roman Empire and the Catholic Church, the Catholic Church being a kind of spiritual empire, which transcends (without abolishing) nationalities in a

---

[1] Aidan Nichols, *The Realm: An Unfashionable Essay on the Conversion of England* (Oxford: Family Publications, 2008), 23–4.

way partially analogous to that of temporal empires. For both Jones and Waugh their interest in the period of the decline of the Roman Empire is related to their belief that they are witnessing the decline, not only of the British Empire, but of Western civilization more generally. Civilizational decline is not a theme for Spark, but in *The Mandelbaum Gate* archaeology is an important image pointing to the way culture and identity are formed by an accumulation of layers over time, an idea closely connected to Jones' emphasis on geology as a metaphor for cultural formation, in *The Anathemata*, for example, and to his archaeological interests shown in *The Anathemata* and 'The Sleeping Lord'. The archaeological theme is also present in Helena's digging for the Cross in the many-layered Jerusalem. Unlike Jones and Waugh, Spark does not make British history a theme in the works discussed here.

What all three have in common, as has been argued through the above presentation, is a conceptual framework, informed by their Catholicism, which includes the idea of an ultimately spiritual purpose for individuals and cultures, thus a narrative of the development of both individual and cultural identities, which leads to a permanent value attaching to every element which contributes to that goal-directed journey of development. They also recognize and emphasize the coexistence of spiritual and physical worlds, with both levels seen as legitimate and necessary, the spiritual providing the sense of goal, and making itself known through the physical. Jones theorizes the way that the spiritual realm is seen through the physical in his theory of signs in art and in the sacraments; Waugh illustrates it in *Helena* in the significance of the Cross, which Helena finds; and Spark illustrates it in *The Mandelbaum Gate* in the importance of the pilgrimage sites for Barbara's sense of the reality of biblical events. Waugh and Spark both present the importance of the journey of the individual out of the self in love, in the cases of Helena, Guy Crouchback and Barbara Vaughan, whereas Jones concentrates rather on the movement of world history towards Christianity, and of humans in general towards spiritual salvation. All three set out to address conflicts in identity, religious and national (Catholic versus non-Catholic, other diverse elements within British culture against each other), and it is the dynamic and teleological quality of their world-view which allows them to achieve the inclusiveness in their visions on the basis of which they can be said to have solved the problems they started out with. A transition to inclusiveness can be seen in Helena, who learns to love the crowds in Rome, any of whom might be then, or might later become, members of the Church. It occurs in Guy Crouchback, who learns to forgive others' faults, to live in non-Catholic England, instead of Catholic Italy, and to bring up as a son a boy whose natural father was another man (and a rival for his former wife). Barbara comes to feel that by directing her energies in love towards her future husband, she can combine her background identities into one, all in the context of an overlaid spiritual journey. Jones particularly emphasizes the place of every individual, from any historical period or part of the world, in salvation history, and insists that the divine plan is that no individual should be lost (just as the poet's task is to lose no cultural strand which can be recalled):

> Whoever he was
> *Dona eis requiem sempiternam.*
> (He would not lose him
> ... *non perdidi ex eis quemquam.*)[2]

Jones' (controversial) insistence here on universal salvation might be seen as an anticipation of Hans Urs von Balthasar's insistence that universal salvation must be hoped for.

Chesterton and Greene have been briefly considered to show that the specific theory of cultural reconciliation found in Jones', Waugh's and Spark's work is not inevitably characteristic of British Catholic writers working in the twentieth century, even in the case of writers, like Chesterton and Greene, who do address nationality and religious issues, and who were also personally attracted to continental Europe, as British Catholic writers often are.

---

2   'Give them eternal rest ... I did not lose any one of them'. (my translation) *The Anathemata*, 66 – Jones talking of the creator of a prehistoric artwork.

This study has been an attempt to show that the three authors, Jones, Waugh and Spark, in the works which have been discussed, have not only addressed problems relating to Catholic and British identity, but have also portrayed solutions to these problems. Their very similar solutions draw on traditional Catholic thinking and particularly on aspects of that thinking which figure prominently since Newman – the role of the development of tradition, of tradition as narrative, and of the abiding value of all contributory elements to that tradition. In doing so they have found an approach to cultural diversity which is both orthodox and celebratory.

Bibliography

Aldritt, Keith, *David Jones: Writer and Artist* (London: Constable, 2003).
Allchin, A. M., 'On Not Knowing Welsh: David Jones and the Matter of Wales', *David Jones: Diversity in Unity: Studies in his Literary and Visual Art*, Belinda Humphrey and Anne Price-Owen, eds (Cardiff: University of Wales Press, 2000), 75–82.
Allitt, Patrick, *Catholic Converts: British and American Intellectuals Turn to Rome* (Ithaca, NY: Cornell University Press, 1977).
Balthasar, Hans Urs von, *Epilogue*, trans. by Edward T. Oakes (San Francisco: Ignatius, 2004).
Barker, Dudley, *G. K. Chesterton: A Biography* (London: Constable, 1973).
Baron, Xavier, 'Medieval Arthurian Motifs in the Modernist Art and Poetry of David Jones', *Studies in Medievalism* 4 (1992), 247–69.
Beaty, Frederick L., *The Ironic World of Evelyn Waugh: A Study of Eight Novels* (De Kalb, IL: Northern Illinois University Press, 1992).
Blamires, David, *David Jones: Artist and Writer* (Manchester: Manchester University Press, 1971).
——, 'Roma Aurea Roma in the Writings of David Jones', *Anglo-Welsh Review* 22.50 (Autumn 1973), 44–57.
Blissett, William, *The Long Conversation: A Memoir of David Jones* (Oxford: Oxford University Press, 1981).
——, 'The Welsh Thing in Here', *David Jones, Artist and Poet*, Paul Hills, ed. (Aldershot: Scolar Press, 1997), 101–21.
Bold, Alan, *Muriel Spark* (London: Methuen, 1986).
Brennan, Michael G., 'Graham Greene, Evelyn Waugh and Mexico', *Renascence* 55, No. 1, Fall 2002, 5–23.
——, *Graham Greene: Fictions, Faith and Authorship* (London: Continuum, 2010).
Calder, Angus, 'Introduction', *Sword of Honour*, Evelyn Waugh (London: Penguin, 1999), vii–xxviii.
Caporaletti, Silvana, *A World in a Grain of Sand: I romanzi di Muriel Spark* (Lecce: Milella, 2000).
Carceller Guillamet, Ma Eulàlia, 'Religion and Reconciliation in *Helena*', *Waugh Without End: New Trends in Evelyn Waugh Studies*, Carlos Villar Flor and Robert Murray Davis, eds (Bern: Peter Lang, 2005), 211–23.

Carens, James F., *The Satiric Art of Evelyn Waugh* (Seattle: University of Washington Press, 1966).

Carr, Helen, 'Modernism and Travel (1880–1940)', *The Cambridge Companion to Travel Writing*, Peter Hulme and Tim Youngs, eds (Cambridge: Cambridge University Press, 2002), 70–86.

Carruthers, Gerard, 'Muriel Spark as Catholic Novelist', *The Edinburgh Companion to Muriel Spark*, Michael Gardiner and Willy Maley, eds (Cambridge: Cambridge University Press, 2010), 74–84.

Chesterton, G. K., *The Autobiography of G. K. Chesterton* (San Francisco: Ignatius, 2006).

——, *The Collected Poems of G. K. Chesterton* (London: Methuen, 1950).

——, *Geoffrey Chaucer* (London: House of Stratus, 2000).

——, *The Innocence of Father Brown* (London: Penguin, 1950).

——, *Irish Impressions* (Norfolk, VA: IHS Press, 2002).

——, *The Napoleon of Notting Hill* (Oxford: Oxford University Press, 1994).

——, *A Short History of England* (Teddington: Echo Library, 2008).

Cheyette, Bryan, *Muriel Spark* (Tavistock: Northcote House, 2000).

——, 'Writing Against Conversion: Muriel Spark and the Gentile Jewesses', *Theorizing Muriel Spark: Gender, Race, Deconstruction*, Martin McQuillan, ed. (London: Palgrave, 2002), 95–112.

Cook, William J., *Masks, Modes and Morals: The Art of Evelyn Waugh* (Rutherford, NJ: Fairleigh Dickinson University Press, 1971).

Corcoran, Neil, *The Song of Deeds: A Study of* The Anathemata *of David Jones* (Cardiff: University of Wales Press, 1982).

Coren, Michael, *Gilbert: The Man Who Was G. K. Chesterton* (London: Jonathan Cape, 1989).

Cunningham, Valentine, *British Writers of the Thirties* (Oxford: Oxford University Press, 1988).

Davenport, Guy, 'Stanley Spencer and David Jones', *Craft and Tradition: Essays in Honour of William Blissett*, H. B. de Groot and Alexander Legatt, eds (Calgary: University of Calgary Press, 1990), 259–68.

Davis, Robert Murray, *Evelyn Waugh and the Forms of his Time* (Washington, DC: Catholic University Press of America, 1989).

——, *Evelyn Waugh, Writer* (Norman, OK: Pilgrim Books, 1981).

——, 'The Rhetoric of Mexican Travel: Greene and Waugh', *Renascence* 38. 3 (Spring 1986), 160–9.

De Vitis, A. A., *Roman Holiday: The Catholic Novels of Evelyn Waugh* (London: Vision Press, 1958).

Dilworth, Thomas, 'David Jones and the Maritain Conversation', *David Jones: Diversity in Unity: Studies in his Literary and Visual Art*, Belinda Humphrey and Anne Price-Owen, eds (Cardiff: University of Wales Press, 2000), 43–55.
——, *David Jones in the Great War* (London: Enitharmion Press, 2012).
——, *Reading David Jones* (Cardiff: University of Wales Press, 2008).
——, *The Shape of Meaning in the Poetry of David Jones* (Toronto: University of Toronto Press, 1988).
Dorenkamp, Angela G., 'Time and Sacrament in *The Anathemata*', *Renascence* 23.4 (Summer 1971), 183–91.
Dunne, Joseph, *Back to the Rough Ground: 'Phronesis' and 'Techne' in Modern Philosophy and in Aristotle* (Notre Dame, IN: University of Notre Dame Press, 1992).
Edgecombe, Rodney Stenning, *Vocation and Identity in the Fiction of Muriel Spark* (Columbia: University of Missouri Press, 1990).
Evans, Geraint, 'Images of National Renewal in "The Sleeping Lord"', *David Jones: Diversity in Unity: Studies in his Literary and Visual Art*, Belinda Humphrey and Anne Price-Owen, eds (Cardiff: University of Wales Press, 2000), 83–90.
Everatt, A. C., 'Doing and Making', *David Jones: Diversity in Unity: Studies in his Literary and Visual Art*, Belinda Humphrey and Anne Price-Owen, eds (Cardiff: University of Wales Press, 2000), 65–74.
Fussell, Paul, *Abroad: British Literary Travelling Between the Wars* (Oxford: Oxford University Press, 1982).
Gallagher, Donat, 'The Humanizing Factor: Evelyn Waugh's "Very Personal View of Providence"', *Waugh Without End: New Trends in Evelyn Waugh Studies*, Carlos Villar Flor and Robert Murray Davis, eds (Bern: Peter Lang, 2005), 21–36.
Greene, Graham, *Brighton Rock* (London: Vintage, 2004).
——, *A Life in Letters*, Richard Greene, ed. (London: Abacus, 2007).
——, *A Sort of Life* (London: Vintage, 1999).
Griffiths, Richard, *The Pen and the Cross: Catholicism and English Literature 1850–2000* (London: Continuum, 2010).
Hague, René, *David Jones* (Cardiff: University of Wales Press, 1975).
Hastings, Selina, *Evelyn Waugh: A Biography* (London: Minerva, 1995).
Hooker, Jeremy, 'David Jones and the Matter of Wales', *David Jones: Diversity in Unity: Studies in his Literary and Visual Art*, Belinda Humphrey and Anne Price-Owen, eds (Cardiff: University of Wales Press, 2000), 11–25.
Hopkins, Gerard Manley, *The Major Works*, Catherine Phillips, ed. (Oxford: Oxford University Press, 1986).
Hurley, Michael D., *G. K. Chesterton* (Tavistock: Northcote, 2012).
Hynes, Joseph, *The Art of the Real: Muriel Spark's Novels* (London: Associated University Presses, 1988).

Johnstone, Richard, *The Will to Believe: Novelists of the Nineteen-thirties* (Oxford University Press, 1982).
Jones, David, *The Anathemata: Fragments of an Attempted Writing* (London: Faber, 1972).
——, *Dai Greatcoat: A Self-Portrait of David Jones in his Letters*, René Hague, ed. (London: Faber, 2008).
——, *The Dying Gaul and Other Writings*, Harman Grisewood, ed. (London: Faber, 1978).
——, *Epoch and Artist*, Harman Grisewood, ed. (London: Faber, 1959).
——, *In Parenthesis* (New York: New York Review of Books, 2003).
——, *The Sleeping Lord and Other Fragments* (London: Faber, 1995).
——, *Wedding Poems*, Thomas Dilworth, ed. (London: Enitharmion, 2002).
Judge, Elizabeth, 'Notes on the Outside: David Jones, Unshared Backgrounds and (the Absence of) Canonicity', *Essays in Literary History* 68.1 (Spring 2001), 179–213.
Kavanagh, P. J., 'Chesterton Reappraised', *G. K. Chesterton: Half a Century of Views*, D. J. Conlon, ed. (Oxford: Oxford University Press, 1987), 347–63.
Kellogg, Gene, *The Vital Tradition: The Catholic Novel in a Period of Convergence* (Chicago: Loyola University Press, 1970).
Kemp, Peter, *Muriel Spark* (London: Paul Elek, 1974).
Ker, Ian, *The Catholic Revival in English Literature, 1845–1961: Newman, Hopkins, Belloc, Chesterton, Greene, Waugh* (Leominster: Gracewing, 2003).
——, *G. K. Chesterton: A Biography* (Oxford: Oxford University Press, 2011).
Kermode, Frank, 'The Novel as Jerusalem: Muriel Spark's *The Mandelbaum Gate*', *Modern Essays*, 2nd edn (London: Fontana, 1971), 267–83.
Lewis, Saunders, 'A Note', *Agenda: An Anthology: The First Four Decades (1959–1993)*, William Cookson, ed. (Manchester: Carcanet, 1996), 336–7.
Lewty, Simon, 'The Palimpsest', *David Jones, Artist and Poet*, Paul Hills, ed. (Aldershot: Scolar Press, 1997), 54–64.
Littlewood, Ian, *The Writings of Evelyn Waugh* (Oxford: Blackwell, 1983).
Lodge, David, *Evelyn Waugh* (New York: Columbia University Press, 1971).
——, *Graham Greene* (New York: Columbia University Press, 1966).
Long, J. V., 'The Consolations of Exile: Evelyn Waugh and Catholicism', *Waugh Without End: New Trends in Evelyn Waugh Studies*, Carlos Villar Flor and Robert Murray Davis, eds (Bern: Peter Lang, 2005), 11–20.
McCartney, George, 'The Being and Becoming of Evelyn Waugh', *Evelyn Waugh: New Directions*, Alain Blayac, ed. (Basingstoke: Palgrave Macmillan, 1992), 133–55.
——, *Confused Roaring: Evelyn Waugh and the Modernist Tradition* (Bloomington: Indiana University Press, 1987).

——, 'Helena in Room 101: The Sum of Truth in Waugh and Orwell', *Waugh Without End: New Trends in Evelyn Waugh Studies*, Carlos Villar Flor and Robert Murray Davis, eds (Bern: Peter Lang, 2005), 59–69.
McInerny, Ralph, *Some Catholic Writers* (South Bend, IN: St Augustine's Press, 2007).
MacIntyre, Alasdair, *After Virtue: A Study in Moral Theory*, 2nd edn (London: Duckworth, 1985).
——, 'Epistemological Crises, Dramatic Narrative, and the Philosophy of Science', *The Tasks of Philosophy: Selected Essays*, vol. 1 (Cambridge: Cambridge University Press, 2006), 3–23.
——, 'How Can We Learn What *Veritatis Splendor* Has to Teach?', *The Thomist*, 58.2 (1994), 191–4.
——, *Three Rival Versions of Moral Enquiry: Encyclopaedia, Genealogy, and Tradition* (Notre Dame, IN: University of Notre Dame Press, 1990).
——, *Whose Justice? Which Rationality?* (Notre Dame, Indiana: University of Notre Dame Press, 1988).
Malin, Irving, 'The Deceptions of Muriel Spark', *The Vision Obscured: Perceptions of Some Twentieth-Century Catholic Novelists*, Melvin J. Friedman, ed. (New York: Fordham University Press, 1970), 95–107.
Malkoff, Karl, *Muriel Spark* (New York: Columbia University Press, 1968).
Massie, Allan, *Muriel Spark* (Edinburgh: Ramsey Head, 1979).
Milbank, Alison, *Chesterton and Tolkien as Theologians: The Fantasy of the Real* (London: T & T Clark, 2007).
Miles, Peter, 'The Writer at the Takutu River: Nature, Art, and Modernist Discourse in Evelyn Waugh's Travel Writing', *Studies in Travel Writing* 18. 1 (2004), 65–87.
Myers, William, *Evelyn Waugh and the Problem of Evil* (London: Faber, 1991).
Newman, John Henry, *An Essay in Aid of a Grammar of Assent* (Notre Dame, IN: University of Notre Dame Press, 1979).
——, *An Essay on the Development of Christian Doctrine* (Notre Dame, IN: University of Notre Dame Press, 1989).
——, *Fifteen Sermons Preached Before the University of Oxford Between A.D. 1826 and 1843* (Notre Dame, IN: University of Notre Dame Press, 1997).
Nichols, Aidan, *Discovering Aquinas: An Introduction to his Life, Work and Influence* (London: Darton, Longman and Todd, 2002).
——, *The Realm: An Unfashionable Essay on the Conversion of England* (Oxford: Family Publications, 2008).
——, *Redeeming Beauty: Soundings in Sacral Aesthetics* (Aldershot: Ashgate, 2007).
Oddie, William, *Chesterton and the Romance of Orthodoxy: The Making of GKC 1874–1908* (Oxford: Oxford University Press, 2008).

Oser, Lee, *The Return of Christian Humanism: Chesterton, Eliot, Tolkien, and the Romance of History* (Columbia: University of Missouri Press, 2007).

Pacey, Philip, *David Jones and Other Wonder Voyagers: Essays by Philip Pacey* (Bridgend: Poetry Wales Press, 1982).

Page, Norman, *Muriel Spark* (London: Macmillan, 1990).

Pagnoulle, Christine, *David Jones: A Commentary on some Poetic Fragments* (Cardiff: University of Wales Press, 1987).

Patey, Douglas Lane, *The Life of Evelyn Waugh: A Critical Biography* (Oxford: Blackwell, 1998).

Pearce, Joseph, 'The Catholic Literary Revival', *From Without the Flaminian Gate: 150 Years of Roman Catholicism in England and Wales, 1850–2000*, V. Allan McClelland and Michael Hodgetts, eds (London: Darton, Longman and Todd, 1999).

——, *Literary Converts: Spiritual Inspiration in an Age of Unbelief* (London: HarperCollins, 1999).

——, *Wisdom and Innocence: A Life of G. K. Chesterton* (London: Hodder and Stoughton, 1996).

Piette, Adam, 'Travel Writing and the Imperial Subject in 1930s Prose: Waugh, Bowen, Smith, and Orwell', *Issues in Travel Writing: Empire, Spectacle, and Displacement*, Kristi Siegel, ed. (New York: Peter Lang, 2002), 53–65.

Piggott, Stuart, 'David Jones and the Past of Man', *Agenda: An Anthology: The First Four Decades (1959–1993)*, William Cookson, ed. (Manchester: Carcanet, 1996), 332–5.

Poitou, Marc, 'La rage d'être autre: *The Mandelbaum Gate* de Muriel Spark', *Cycnos* 2 (Hiver 1985–6), 17–25.

Potter, Martin, 'Catholic Approaches to Jerusalem: Fragmentation and Continuity of Identities – Evelyn Waugh's *Helena* and Muriel Spark's *The Mandelbaum Gate*', *Topodynamics of Arrival: Essays on Self and Pilgrimage*, Gert Hofmann and Snježana Zorić, eds (Amsterdam: Rodopi, 2012), 115–38.

——, 'East versus West: Latin and Byzantine Civilisation Contrasted in Evelyn Waugh's *Helena*', *Romanian Journal of English Studies* 7, 2010, 233–40.

——, 'Reconciling the Divided Self in Muriel Spark's *The Mandelbaum Gate*', *University of Bucharest Review* 10.1, 2008, 40–6.

——, 'Transformations and Transfigurations: Britishness and Romanness Across the Epochs in Evelyn Waugh and David Jones', *University of Bucharest Review* 11.2 (2009), 115–21.

Prescott, Lynda, 'Greene, Waugh and the Lure of Travel', *Books Without Borders, Volume 1: The Cross-National Dimension in Print Culture*, Robert Fraser and Mary Hammond, eds (Basingstoke: Palgrave, 2008).

Price, Alan, *Brighton Rock (Graham Greene)* (Oxford: Blackwell, 1969).

Richardson, Laurence, *Newman's Approach to Knowledge* (Leominster: Gracewing, 2007).
Robichaud, Paul, *Making the Past Present: David Jones, the Middle Ages, and Modernity* (Washington, DC: Catholic University of America Press, 2007).
Robson, William Wallace, 'Father Brown and Others', *G. K. Chesterton: A Centenary Appraisal* (London: Paul Elek, 1974), 58–72.
Schwartz, Adam, *The Third Spring: G. K. Chesterton, Graham Greene, Christopher Dawson and David Jones* (Washington, DC: Catholic University of America Press, 2005).
Sharrock, Roger, *Saints, Sinners and Comedians: The Novels of Graham Greene* (Tunbridge Wells: Burns and Oates, 1984).
Shelden, Michael, *Graham Greene: The Man Within* (London: Heinemann, 1994).
Sherry, Norman, *The Life of Graham Greene*, 3 vols (London: Jonathan Cape, 1989–2004).
Spark, Muriel, *The Comforters* (London: Penguin, 1963).
——, *The Complete Short Stories* (London: Penguin, 2002).
——, *Curriculum Vitae: A Volume of Autobiography* (London: Penguin, 1993).
——, 'Edinburgh-born', *Critical Essays on Muriel Spark*, Joseph Hynes, ed. (New York: G. K. Hall, 1992), 21–3.
——, *The Mandelbaum Gate* (London: Penguin, 1967).
——, 'My Conversion', *Critical Essays on Muriel Spark*, Joseph Hynes, ed. (New York: G. K. Hall, 1992), 24–8.
——, *The Prime of Miss Jean Brodie* (London: Penguin, 1965).
Sproxton, Judy, *The Women of Muriel Spark* (London: Constable, 1992).
Stannard, Martin, 'Debunking the Jungle: The Context of Evelyn Waugh's Travel Books: 1930–9', *Prose Studies* 5.1 (May 1982), 105–26.
——, *Muriel Spark: The Biography* (London: Weidenfeld and Nicholson, 2009).
Staudt, Kathleen Henderson, *At the Turn of a Civilization: David Jones and Modern Poetics* (Ann Arbor: University of Michigan Press, 1994).
Taylor, Charles, *Sources of the Self: The Making of Modern Identity* (Cambridge: Cambridge University Press, 1989).
Walczuk, Anna, *Irony as a Mode of Perception and Principle of Ordering Reality in the Novels of Muriel Spark* (Krakow: Universitas, 2008).
Ward, Elizabeth, *David Jones: Mythmaker* (Manchester: Manchester University Press, 1983).
Watts, Cedric, *Darkest Greeneland*: Brighton Rock (Berkhamsted: Graham Greene Birthplace Trust, 1999).
Waugh, Evelyn, *Brideshead Revisited* (London: Penguin, 1962).
——, *Decline and Fall* (London: Penguin, 1989).

—, *The Diaries of Evelyn Waugh*, Michael Davie, ed. (London: Penguin, 1979).
—, *A Handful of Dust* (London: Penguin, 1997).
—, *Helena* (London: Penguin, 1963).
—, *Labels: A Mediterranean Journal* (London: Penguin, 1985).
—, *A Little Learning* (London: Penguin, 1983).
—, *A Little Order: A Selection from his Journalism*, Donat Gallagher, ed. (London: Eyre Methuen, 1977).
—, *Ninety-Two Days: Travels in Guiana and Brazil* (London: Serif, 2007).
—, *Remote People* (London: Penguin, 2002).
—, *Robbery Under Law: The Mexican Object-Lesson* (Pleasantville, NY: Akadine, 1999).
—, *Sword of Honour* (London: Penguin, 1999).
—, *A Tourist in Africa* (London: Methuen, 1985).
—, *Two Lives: Edmund Campion – Ronald Knox* (London: Continuum, 2001).
—, *When the Going was Good* (London: Penguin, 1951).
Whitehead, Neil L., 'South America/Amazonia: The Forest of Marvels', *The Cambridge Companion to Travel Writing*, Peter Hulme and Tim Youngs, eds (Cambridge: Cambridge University Press, 2002), 122–38.
Whittacker, Ruth, *The Faith and Fiction of Muriel Spark* (London: Macmillan, 1982).
Wilcockson, Colin, 'David Jones and "The Break"', *Agenda* 15.2–3 (1977), 126–31.
Williams, Rowan, *Grace and Necessity: Reflections on Art and Love* (London: Continuum, 2005).
Woodman, Thomas, *Faithful Fictions: The Catholic Novel in British Literature* (Milton Keynes: Open University Press, 1991).
Wykes, David, *Evelyn Waugh: A Literary Life* (Basingstoke: Macmillan, 1999).

Index

Aneirin 16, 24
Anglicanism 2, 4–5, 79, 92, 104, 105, 106–8, 137
Aquinas 6, 31
archaeology 123, 140
Aristotle 6
Arthur 16–17, 23, 26, 33, 38, 41, 42, 50, 53
Augustine 6, 34, 45, 61, 120

Bendigeid Vran 21
Brân 14, 26, 38
British culture 3, 25, 27, 31, 34, 36, 39, 40, 51, 54, 137, 140
British Empire 4, 35, 43, 45–7, 60, 64, 67, 70–1, 74, 79, 139–40
British Guiana (Guyana) 58–60
British identity 3–4, 136, 137, 138, 139, 142
   Chesterton 129–30
   Greene 134, 136
   Jones 23–7
   Spark 116
   Waugh 83, 87–8, 129, 132

Calvinism 2, 60, 91–102
Campion, Edmund 64–5
Chesterton, G. K. 8, 78, 125–33
   Autobiography 127
   Geoffrey Chaucer (*GC*) 131–3
   Innocence of Father Brown, The 127–8
   Irish Impressions (*II*) 128
   life 126
   Napoleon of Notting Hill, The 127
   Short History of England, A (*SHE*) 129–30

Coel *see* Cole
Cole, King 33, 38, 68, 72–4
Constantine 67–8, 76, 78, 80
Constantius Chlorus 67–8, 70–2, 73–6, 77
conversion 4, 5, 77–8, 105, 109, 111, 123
   Chesterton 126, 128
   Greene 133
   Jones 12
   Spark 89, 93, 102, 122
   Waugh 55, 56, 79, 82
Coptic Church 81
Culhwch ac Olwen 24, 25, 50
Cunedda Wledig 14, 52

Edinburgh 90, 91–2, 93–102
empiricism 39, 69–70, 76, 77, 78, 80, 82–3, 129, 132
English culture 17, 22–7, 72
English identity 3–4, 128–32, 134, 136, 137–9
   Chesterton 126
   Greene 133
   Jones 10, 16, 28, 30, 39, 49, 54, 137
   Spark 90–3, 94–5, 98, 102, 104, 106, 112–13, 116–17
   Waugh 56, 59–63, 65, 66–7, 69, 70, 74, 85
Englynion y Beddau 24
Ethiopian Church 63, 81
Eucharist 18–19, 33, 40, 42, 50, 107

First World War 1, 10, 12, 13, 21–7, 45, 46, 47, 53, 127, 130, 138

geography 13, 21, 22, 34, 35, 36, 42, 51
geology 17, 27, 32, 33, 39, 51, 140
Gill, Eric 11
Greene, Graham 7–8, 57, 58, 133–6
   Brighton Rock (*BR*) 8, 134–6
   Honorary Consul, The 134
   life 133
   Our Man in Havana 134
   Power and the Glory, The 134

Helen 15, 26, 39
Historia Brittonum 28
Holy Land 42, 105–23
Hopkins, Gerard Manley 17, 24, 43, 45

industrialization 11, 13, 44, 52–3
Irish culture 25
Irish identity 130–1
Italian culture 94, 96
Italian fascism 94
Italian identity 64, 84–6, 88, 138, 139

Jerusalem 26, 33, 42, 44, 46, 47, 68, 81, 106, 110, 113, 115–16, 119–21, 140
Jewish identity 90, 91, 92–3, 103–22, 137, 138, 139
Jones, David 1, 3–4, 6, 8, 9–54, 55, 67, 75, 137–42
   Anathemata, The (*TA*) 27–43, 51, 54, 140
   Dai Greatcoat (*Dai G*) 10–12
   Dying Gaul, The (*The DG*) 10, 12
   Epoch and Artist (*EA*) 10, 12
   In Parenthesis (*IP*) 21–7, 36, 45, 54, 138
   life 10–12
   Sleeping Lord, The (*SL*) 41, 43–54, 140
   Wedding Poems (*WP*) 51
Joyce, James 16, 20, 30

Latin 25, 29, 41, 47, 86
Lewis, Saunders 3 n.4, 25 n.17, 44
liturgy 12, 25, 31, 32, 33, 39–42, 48, 81
Llywelyn ap Gruffydd 12, 13
London 10, 14, 21, 24, 27, 28, 34, 37–40, 44, 45, 51, 106–7, 127

MacIntyre, Alasdair 6–7
Malory 24, 24 n.16
Maritain, Jacques 11, 11 n.6
Mass 33, 36, 40, 42, 108, 120
Mexico 58, 61–3
Middle Ages 3, 12, 13, 23, 24, 35, 70, 127

national identity 1, 3–4, 7–8, 125, 136, 139, 140, 141
   Chesterton 127, 130–3
   Greene 136
   Jones 9, 12, 17, 19–20, 26, 28, 36, 40–1, 43, 44, 50, 54
   Spark 89, 90, 93, 94, 97, 101–2, 122–3
   Waugh 55, 56, 57, 63, 64, 67, 68, 79, 86
   see also British identity, English identity, Irish identity, Italian identity, Jewish identity, Scottish identity, Welsh identity
Newman, John Henry 4–5, 100, 105, 122

Old Norse 48
Orthodox Church 76, 121
Oxford 41

Post-Impressionism 18
Protestantism 2 n.1, 3, 137
   Chesterton 132
   Greene 136
   Jones 15
   Spark 95, 97, 122
   Waugh 58, 62, 64, 65

Reformation 1, 2, 3, 43, 65, 131, 132
Rhodes, Cecil 64
Roman Britain 3
  Jones 15, 16, 25–6, 36, 38–9, 40–1, 47–9
  Waugh 67, 72–3
Roman Empire 4, 139–40
  Jones 13–15, 27, 34, 36, 40–3, 44–7, 49–50, 51
  Waugh 67, 67 n.27, 70–1, 73, 74–5, 78, 79, 86, 87
Romanticism 8, 95, 96, 100, 101, 125, 127, 130
Rome 141
  Jones 14 n.7, 15, 34, 44, 47, 48
  Spark 120–1
  Waugh 68, 70, 73, 74, 77, 78–80, 81 n.33, 82

Scottish identity 3–4, 54, 90, 91, 126, 136, 139
Second World War 38, 55, 71, 76, 84, 89
Shakespeare 24, 38, 47, 72, 73
slang 23–4, 46, 69, 71–2
Spark, Muriel 2, 6, 8, 55, 89–123, 137–42
  Comforters, The 89
  Curriculum Vitae (*CV*) 90–3, 102, 103, 139
  'Gentile Jewesses, The' (*GJ*) 90, 93, 102, 103–5
  life 89–93
  Mandelbaum Gate, The (*MG*) 88, 92, 93, 98, 102, 103, 104, 105–23, 138, 139, 140
  Prime of Miss Jean Brodie, The (*PMJB*) 90, 93–102
Spengler 15, 20, 35, 41 n.31, 42, 45, 49

Taliesin 25, 25 n.17
Thomism 4, 6, 11, 35
Triads 24
Troy 25, 33, 34, 44, 52–3, 69

Waugh, Evelyn 3–4, 6, 8, 55–88, 137–42
  Brideshead Revisited (*BR*) 57, 65–7, 84
  Decline and Fall 56
  Handful of Dust, A 60–1
  Helena (*Hel*) 15, 36, 44, 46, 56, 65, 67–83, 84, 86, 87, 129, 139, 140
  Labels 57
  life 56
  Little Learning, A (*LL*) 56
  Ninety-Two Days (*NTD*) 58–60, 79
  Ordeal of Gilbert Pinfold, The 89
  Remote People 58, 81
  Robbery Under Law (*RUL*) 61–3
  Sword of Honour (*SH*) 76, 77, 83–8, 138
  Tourist in Africa, A (*TA*) 63–4
  Two Lives (*TL*) 64–5
  Waugh in Abyssinia (*WA*) 58, 63
  When the Going was Good (*WGG*) 57
Welsh culture 13–14, 15, 16, 21–7, 33, 38, 39, 43, 44, 47, 49, 50, 52, 72–3, 139
Welsh identity 3–4, 137, 138, 139
  Jones 10–17, 20, 21–7, 28, 30, 32, 33, 38, 39, 42, 43, 54
  Waugh 56, 68–70, 72–3
Welsh language 10–11, 13, 16, 29, 32, 41, 47, 49, 50, 51, 52
Widsith 25

Y Gododdin 16, 24, 33

Cultural Identity Studies

Edited by
Helen Chambers

This series aims to publish new research (monographs and essays) into relationships and interactions between culture and identity. The notions of both culture and identity are broadly conceived; interdisciplinary and theoretically diverse approaches are encouraged in a series designed to promote a better understanding of the processes of identity formation, both individual and collective. It will embrace research into the roles of linguistic, social, political, psychological, and religious factors, taking account of historical context. Work on the theorizing of cultural aspects of identity formation, together with case studies of individual writers, thinkers or cultural products will be included. It focuses primarily on cultures linked to European languages, but welcomes transcultural links and comparisons. It is published in association with the Institute of European Cultural Identity Studies of the University of St Andrews.

Vol. 1   Helen Chambers (ed.)
         Violence, Culture and Identity: Essays on German and
         Austrian Literature, Politics and Society. 436 pages. 2006.
         ISBN 3-03910-266-4 / US-ISBN 0-8204-7195-X

Vol. 2   Heather Williams
         Postcolonial Brittany: Literature between Languages. 191 pages. 2007.
         ISBN 978-3-03-910556-4 / US-ISBN 978-0-8204-7583-7

Vol. 3   Andrew Hiscock (ed.)
         Mighty Europe 1400–1700: Writing an Early Modern Continent.
         240 pages. 2007.
         ISBN 978-3-03911-074-2

Vol. 4   Marie-Claire Patron
         Culture and Identity in Study Abroad Contexts: After Australia,
         French without France. 332 pages. 2007.
         ISBN 978-3-03911-082-7

Vol. 5   Henriëtte Louwerse
         Homeless Entertainment: On Hafid Bouazza's Literary Writing.
         252 pages. 2007.
         ISBN 978-3-03911-333-0

Vol. 6   Robbie Aitken
         Exclusion and Inclusion, Gradations of Whiteness and Socio-
         Economic Engineering in German Southwest Africa, 1884-1914.
         265 pages. 2007.
         ISBN 978-3-03911-060-5

Vol. 7   Lorna Milne (ed.)
         Postcolonial Violence, Culture and Identity in Francophone Africa
         and the Antilles. 233 pages. 2007.
         ISBN 978-3-03910-330-0

Vol. 8   David Gascoigne (ed.)
         Violent Histories: Violence, Culture and Identity in France from
         Surrealism to the Néo-polar. 204 pages. 2007.
         ISBN 978-3-03910-317-1

Vol. 9   Victoria Carpenter (ed.)
         A World Torn Apart: Representations of Violence in
         Latin American Narrative. 304 pages. 2007.
         ISBN 978-3-03911-335-4

Vol. 10   Georg Grote
         The South Tyrol Question, 1866–2010: From National Rage to
         Regional State. 194 pages. 2012.
         ISBN 978-3-03911-336-1

Vol. 11   Áine McGillicuddy
         René Schickele and Alsace: Cultural Identity between the Borders.
         302 pages. 2011.
         ISBN 978-3-03911-393-4

Vol. 12 Irene Gilsenan Nordin and Carmen Zamorano Llena (eds)
Redefinitions of Irish Identity: A Postnationalist Approach.
310 pages. 2010.
ISBN 978-3-03911-558-7

Vol. 13 Elisabeth Lillie (ed.)
Sense and Sensitivity: Difference and Diversity in Higher Education Classrooms. 260 pages. 2013.
ISBN 978-3-03911-869-4

Vol. 14 Philip Dine
Sport and Identity in France: Practices, Locations, Representations.
383 pages. 2012.
ISBN 978-3-03911-898-4

Vol. 15 George McKay, Christopher Williams, Michael Goddard, Neil Foxlee and Egidija Ramanauskaitė (eds)
Subcultures and New Religious Movements in Russia and East-Central Europe. 453 pages. 2009.
ISBN 978-3-03911-921-9

Vol. 16 Katia Pizzi and Godela Weiss-Sussex (eds)
The Cultural Identities of European Cities. 249 pages. 2011.
ISBN 978-3-03911-930-1

Vol. 17 Kevin Searle
From Farms to Foundries: An Arab Community in Industrial Britain.
255 pages. 2010.
ISBN 978-3-03911-934-9

Vol. 18 Paul Gifford and Tessa Hauswedell (eds)
Europe and its Others: Essays on Interperception and Identity.
305 pages. 2010.
ISBN 978-3-03911-968-4

Vol. 19 Philip Dine and Seán Crosson (eds)
Sport, Representation and Evolving Identities in Europe.
408 pages. 2010.
ISBN 978-3-03911-977-6

Vol. 20   Forthcoming

Vol. 21   Patrick O'Donovan and Laura Rascaroli (eds)
          The Cause of Cosmopolitanism: Dispositions, Models, Transformations.
          428 pages. 2011.
          ISBN 978-3-0343-0139-8

Vol. 22   Rob Garbutt
          The Locals: Identity, Place and Belonging in Australia and Beyond.
          272 pages. 2011.
          ISBN 978-3-0343-0154-1

Vol. 23   Rossella M. Riccobono (ed.)
          The Poetics of the Margins: Mapping Europe from the Interstices.
          225 pages. 2011.
          ISBN 978-3-0343-0158-9

Vol. 24   Andrew Liston
          The Ecological Voice in Recent German-Swiss Prose.
          248 pages. 2011.
          ISBN 978-3-0343-0218-0

Vol. 25   Nóra de Buiteléir
          Tyrol or Not Tyrol: Theatre as History in Südtirol/Alto Adige.
          233 pages. 2013.
          ISBN 978-3-0343-0731-4

Vol. 26   Kamakshi P. Murti
          To Veil or not to Veil: Europe's Shape-Shifting 'Other'.
          247 pages. 2013.
          ISBN 978-3-0343-0859-5

Vol. 27   Martin Potter
          British and Catholic? National and Religious Identity in the Work of
          David Jones, Evelyn Waugh and Muriel Spark.
          161 pages. 2013.
          ISBN 978-3-0343-0860-1